THREADS OF THINKING

THREADS OF THINKING

Young children learning
and the role of early education

Cathy Nutbrown

Second Edition

P·C·P
Paul Chapman
Publishing Ltd

Copyright © 1999, Cathy Nutbrown

First edition published 1994
Second edition published 1999

Paul Chapman Publishing Ltd
A SAGE Publications Company
6 Bonhill Street
London EC2A 4PU

SAGE Publications Inc
2455 Teller Road
Thousand Oaks, California 91320

SAGE Publications India Pvt Ltd
32, M-Block Market
Greater Kailash - I
New Delhi 110 048

British Library Cataloguing in Publication data

A catalogue record for this book is available from the British Library

ISBN 1 85396 458 1
ISBN 1 85396 459 X (pbk)

Library of Congress catalog card number available

Typeset by Dorwyn Ltd, Rowlands Castle, Hants
Printed and bound by Athenaeum Press Ltd, Newcastle upon Tyne

For
my daughter
with love
September 1998

If we think of learning as part of growth, and if we are concerned with the quality of growth and fulfilment of growth, we must define our purpose in terms which relate to these ideas and use words which relate to our thoughts. Our thoughts are always imprisoned within the words we use to express them, and we cannot solve a problem if we use the wrong language. We have need to use the language not of building and mechanics but of biology – roots, nourishment, growth – since we are concerned not with machines but with living, growing beings. If we think in terms of how children grow roots, into what they grow roots, and how these roots can best be nourished, we must use words which express such ideas.

Christian Schiller

CONTENTS

ACKNOWLEDGEMENTS

During my years as a teacher of young children, and during my work with parents, teachers, other early childhood educators, students and researchers, I have met and worked in different ways with many different people. Dialogue and the sharing of thoughts, feelings and ideas shapes everyone's thinking, and it is the richness of interactions which have given shape to my work. I thank those adults and children who, through their contact with me, have given me things to think about, questions to ponder, suggestions and ideas to develop. Some of those people will necessarily remain anonymous, others I am privileged to name.

This second edition builds on the first and so I wish to record again my thanks to those who gave me so much support during 1993 whilst *Threads of Thinking* first came into being. I am grateful to Chris Athey for her professional support, her comments on the original manuscript and for so generously sharing her ground-breaking work which stimulated and challenged my thinking. Tricia David, Mary Jane Drummond, Ann Hedley and Kath Hirst willingly shared in the early processes of writing *Threads of Thinking*. They commented on the developing text in their distinctly creative ways. Their roles were critical to my thinking and I prize my continued connections with them all.

Judi Duffield is one of those exceptional human beings for whom nothing is too much, and I thank her for her contribution to my work and to the making of this second edition of *Threads of Thinking*. I am privileged to work alongside many supportive (and challenging) colleagues in the Department of Educational Studies at the University of Sheffield and I am proud to acknowledge their distinctive, individual and collective contributions to this book.

The other team which has helped to make *Threads of Thinking* what it is includes Marianne Lagrange, Joyce Lynch, Beth Crockett and Paul Chapman: a unique group of people and a publishing team that makes writing books irresistible!

There are times when the act of writing finds me alone in my room tapping at my keyboard, but I rarely write 'alone'. Much of my thinking about and for writing takes place in the enriching company of others. Writing for me is not a solitary process but an intensely human experience of engagement with people and with ideas. I am for ever grateful for the company of those who surround me, and for the love of those most special.

INTRODUCTION

This book is about young children and their educators working together. It is primarily about the promotion of high-quality thinking and action of children aged 3–5 years, though thoughts about younger and older children are also included as part of the discussion of continuity in teaching and learning.

Throughout the book I have used examples of children's talk, action, representation and thinking drawn from observations made over ten years of teaching to illustrate some aspects of their schemas, to demonstrate their capacity as learners and to suggest ways of developing practice in the education of young children. This kind of data could have been used and analysed in many different ways. The interpretations given here are my way of making sense of the complexity of children's behaviour as they grow and learn. In any book of this kind there is room for debate and the many observations have been included for readers to consider my conclusions.

Most of the observations in this book were made in nursery education settings; others draw on children 'in action' at home. It is important that the terms used to describe the adults who work in different contexts with young children are clear. The Rumbold Report (DES, 1990a) tried to overcome this difficulty by using the term 'educator' to apply to everyone who engaged with young children in some way, arguing that all adults, parents, childminders, playgroup workers, teachers, nursery nurses, nannies and so on had a part to play in helping young children to learn. Whilst this attempts to embrace the multidisciplinary nature of work with young children, and the diversity of settings in which they might learn, it makes for a lack of clarity of roles and responsibilities and clouds issues about provision offered and the training, status and qualifications of the people who work with young children. There can also be a dangerous assumption that anyone and everyone can work effectively with young children. If we call everyone involved with young children an 'educator', discussion which separates out distinctive roles, responsibilities and contributions of parents and other educators can become confused, and the specialised nature of the work of different kinds of educators can become blurred or misunderstood. Throughout this book I have tried to overcome this problem in several ways: using specific professional titles to describe adults where they have arisen from certain observations; referring to parents as parents, but acknowledging their important and distinct role in children's learning and development; and referring to educators in a range of group settings as 'professional educators'. I use the term professional educators to mean adults who have relevant training and qualifications, who understand how children learn, and who are active in their thinking and interaction with young children in group settings. In many cases I have referred specifically to teachers because it was those professionals who were involved in the observations described.

This book is intended to provide evidence of children's thinking about, and learning from, their world. It draws, where appropriate, on theories to illuminate the examples of children's language, action and representation. In particular, the work of Athey (1990) is used to explore ways of understanding children's learning.

This book is an attempt to think more deeply about children's actions and interactions and is a voyage of discovery into the riches of children's minds. Here I give my ways of thinking about and working with young children. I invite readers to consider my thoughts and, returning to the children they know best, to make their own observations, develop their own thinking about children's thinking and their own role in the dynamic process of supporting, challenging and extending children's thinking and learning.

Cathy Nutbrown
September 1998

Part I
Young children learning

Our knowledge of young children's cognitive development has been extended by the early work of
Piaget, Vygotsky, Isaacs and other 'Great Educators'
who, in different ways, set out to illustrate the characteristics of children's thinking. Chapter 1 gives
some examples of children trying to make sense of
experiences, and to reason why things happen.
Chapter 2 considers some of Athey's work and deals
with some questions which educators often ask
about schemas and young children's learning.

1
THINKING ABOUT YOUNG CHILDREN LEARNING

Young children cannot be taught effectively if planned learning is always artificially divided into man-made compartments called subjects. Children will, for example, explore science, learn about maths and develop their language through activities and experiences in many different home and community situations as well as through experiences specifically planned for such learning in early education settings.

In the following examples children are learning through realistic and immediate experiences. All the children are using and exploring water, and these observations show how the immediate and engaging experience of playing with water can provide learning opportunities in environments which encourage children to play. Three observations follow, Zoe (aged 4), Ashaq (aged 6) and Karmen and John (aged 8 and 7).

Zoe aged 4

Zoe was playing in the water trough at the nursery. She was experimenting with a jug and water wheel, spending a considerable time filling the jug, pouring the water over the wheel and watching it turn. She poured water at different speeds, and from different heights. Her teacher watched and eventually asked: 'Can you tell me what is happening?' Zoe looked at her and began her explanation: 'The wheel doesn't like to get wet, so it runs fast to get away from the water. When all the water is gone, it stays still again!' Zoe knew that the water made the wheel turn but ascribed attributes of thought and feeling to the wheel. Early experiences of the scientific principles of force, gravity and power are present in this example, as well as the beginnings of reasoned thought. Zoe was beginning to grapple with ideas of speed and of cause, function and effect.

Ashaq aged 6

Ashaq was watching his mother using a jet spray at the garage to wash her car. He observed intently for some time and then asked if he could have a turn. After concentrating the jet of water on one muddy wheel and watch-

3

ing the dirt wash away he said: 'If I put it nearer the dirt goes away faster. That's because the water hits it harder if it doesn't spray so far. If I spray a long way away then not all the dirt goes.'

This 6-year-old told his teacher about the car washing. She used jets, sprays and the advantage of a hot summer day to work with him to develop further this understanding and to extend his interest. Water flowed from the hosepipe in the yard outside the classroom as did questions of 'How?', 'Why?' and 'What if?' Ashaq made reasoned answers to all the questions the teacher raised. He also asked questions of his own. The principles of syphoning were mastered and the appropriate terminology was introduced by the teacher. A small group of children worked purposefully to create and solve their own water-oriented problems.

Learning does not begin and end in school. The visit to the garage with his mother opened up the child's thinking which Ashaq, with the help of his teacher, was able to build on with his peers in school.

Karmen and John aged 8 and 7

Karmen and John were at home in their garden bathing dolls and washing all their clothes. The dolls and clothes were covered in an ever-increasing amount of soap suds. The children had rather overestimated the quantity of washing powder they needed, reasoning that the dolls were extremely dirty and so must need a lot of soap to get them clean. John decided to change the water and wash everything again, this time not putting in any more soap. The following conversation gives an interesting insight into the children's reasoning and understanding:

Karmen: Make the water cooler this time, it disperses the bubbles.
John: How?
Karmen: Not sure, but it does, mum does that with the jumpers in the sink. It sort of pops them.
John: Is it that cold water is too cold for them and it makes them pop?
Karmen: Maybe, it's thinner and gets through the membranes.
John: Brains! Do bubbles have brains?
Karmen: No! Membranes! It's like an invisible sort of film, like a sort of skin thing to keep the air trapped, they have them on *Tomorrow's World* on telly sometimes.
John: How does the air get in there?
Karmen: Well, it's the soap. Get the cold water now.
John: How cold?
Karmen: Cold! Don't put any warm in, though you could put a bit, tepid water, 'hand-hot' my mum calls it I think.
John: Does that mean as hot as my hand?
Karmen: It means you can put your hand in and it doesn't make it red hot or freezing cold so it hurts your fingers.
John: I bet we could do it quicker than changing all this water.
Karmen: How?
John: Stick them all under the tap till all the bubbles run off then squeeze them!

Karmen:	Or! We could use the shower thing in the bathroom and give them a shower. That would work.
John:	I saw that on telly.
Karmen:	What, doing the washing?
John:	No, spraying the oil.
Karmen:	What?
John:	If you spray oil it breaks up, pollutes the environment and the sea, oil does.
Karmen:	Like if you get soap on your hair and use the shower to rinse it off. We'll do the dolls first, their hair is all bubbles.
John:	The particles bombard the oil and hit it to break it up. Dad said.
Karmen:	Does oil have membranes?
John:	Don't know. Give me that jacket. Oil's not as heavy as water though. It floats on top. I saw that on telly too!
Karmen:	We've got brains!
John:	If it works we have. But I bet it does. My mum puts me in the shower on holiday!

Karmen and John were transferring elements of their knowledge gleaned from different sources, including their parents and the television, and using what they knew to try to solve their present difficulty. They were exploring, discovering, checking out each other's meanings, predicting results, forming hypotheses and drawing conclusions. They played co-operatively and with intensity of purpose.

As children get older and more experienced, if adults have spent time with them, extending their interests and explaining things about the world, stimulating their actions and thoughts into new areas, and talking with them, children come to use different language and terminology to explain their reasoning. It is their language which indicates to us their grasp of meaning and their understanding. If children articulate their thinking, their parents, teachers and other educators are in a better position to help them to refine and further develop their ideas.

If we reflect on the use of language in the three examples of children using water we see different thoughts and understandings. Four-year-old Zoe explained: 'It runs away from the water.' Six-year-old Ashaq observed: 'If I put it nearer the dirt goes away faster.' Seven-year-old John said: 'The particles bombard the oil and hit it to break it up.' Eight-year-old Karmen said: 'Membranes, it's like an invisible sort of film; like a sort of skin thing, to keep the air trapped.' If children have played in their earlier years with the stuff of the world (water, sand, mud and clay), they are in a better position to develop further concepts through these media. Children who have had few encounters with these natural materials will need time to explore their properties and attributes so that they can then tackle other challenges and questions when they work with such materials.

Worries about children's safety and urban living now inhibit the freedom of children to explore their world. Concerns for children's well-being include fear of illness from polluted rivers and beaches, and of abduction or

abuse. Adults who wish to support children's learning now bring the stuff
of the world into safe, defined, but falsely created boundaries. The vastness
of the seashore is reduced to small quantities of sand and water in specially
designed containers, and children often wear aprons to protect their
clothing from wet and dirt when part of the learning experience involves
the process of getting sandy, dirty and wet! Instead of making mud pies in
the outdoors, children use small quantities of clay, in a confined space at an
allotted time. The role of the adult in protecting the opportunities for
learning and enabling children's own ways of thinking and exploring is
crucial. Children need the freedom to play and learn, and educators need
to create opportunities which provide this freedom to learn in a protected
environment which, as far as possible, removes the inhibiting restriction
which arises from fear for children's safety. The restrictions which are
placed on children and the consequences of this in terms of their subsequent development were considered by Tinbergen (1976), who discussed
the ways in which young children learn through play in their natural environments. Tinbergen suggested that society has inhibited children's freedom to play and, just as young animals find their own way of learning,
young children could do the same if they were in an appropriate
environment.

John Brierley's contribution to our understanding of children's brain
growth and development provided insights for all who have responsibility
and concerns for young children. Brierley asserted that the years from 0 to
5 are crucial for brain development and that the first ten years are the years
during which the brain reaches 95% of its adult weight. He wrote:

> During these years of swift brain growth a child's eyes, ears and touch
> sense in particular are absorbing experiences of all kinds through
> imitation and exploration. It is obvious that the quality of experience
> is vital for sound development. In addition to sensory experience, talk
> is as vital to human life as pure air.
>
> (Brierley, 1987, p. 28)

Brierley continued to discuss 21 principles for teaching and learning based
upon knowledge of brain development. He made it clear that the more
children learn, the more their brains have the capacity to learn. The following two principles help to focus on implications for young children's learning:

> All forms of play appear to be essential for the intellectual, imagina-
> tive and emotional development of the child and may well be necess-
> ary steps to a further stage of development.
>
> The brain thrives on variety and stimulation. Monotony of surround-
> ings, toys that only do one thing, a classroom display kept up for too
> long are soon disregarded by the brain.
>
> (*Ibid.*, p. 111)

It was variety, stimulation and the important experiences of talking with
adults which prompted the questioning and thinking from the children in
the following two examples. Young thinkers construct some wonderful and

apparently bizarre reasons for why things happen, drawing on their present knowledge to create explanations which are logical to them at that time (Paley, 1981). The following examples illustrate children's skills as thinkers as they struggle to explain and reason things which puzzle them about their world.

A 5-year-old boy asked his parents, 'Why are there trees?' A satisfactory answer took his parents into many reasons and a long discussion which justified the existence of trees: shady places to sit on a hot day; for making wooden furniture; equatorial rain forests; conservation; food and habitats for wildlife; and finally 'somewhere for Robin Hood to hide'. This last reason followed a visit to Sherwood Forest and the Major Oak. One part of the answer led to another question or a further reason and so dialogue between parents and child continued with an interested and lively 5-year-old applying his mind and pursuing this line of thought, continuing to think, assimilate and understand, acquiring more information along the way which extended and further stimulated his thinking. The questioning stopped when, for the moment, he was satisfied with the explanation which had been generated.

A 4-year-old girl asked her father, 'Why does the sea go in and out?' Her father gave the most reasonable explanation he could, mentioning the moon and the spinning of the earth and the need for the sea to come into the harbours of other parts of the world. She thought that the sea came into the harbour of the small town where she lived to let the boats float, and that it went out to stop children swimming in the sea all day so that their skin did not get wrinkled! She thought that this going in and coming out of the sea was all 'a waste of time' and that the sea should stay in the harbour all the time so that the boats could always float and the children could swim whenever they wanted to. Her search for reason and justification led her to create an explanation and some logical reasoning from what she presently knew and how she wanted things to be.

Piaget's insights into children's thought and language contribute to our understanding of young children's minds. Piaget (1953) gave some fascinating lists of 'why' questions which were asked by children, providing illustration of children's thinking and their search for reason. The children about whom Piaget wrote asked questions of causality and questions of justification. Those who spend time with young children will find a familiar tone in questions like 'Why does the sea go in and out?' and 'Why are there trees?' Young children ask questions which Piaget would categorise as 'Whys of logical justification' when they look for logical and sensible reasons for the things they see and are told. Whilst Piaget thought young children 'egocentric', this term need not be considered in a selfish sense, nor should children's egocentricity be thought of as a deficit (Piaget 1972). Young children work hard to make sense of the things they encounter and use all that they know to try to understand. To reply to a child's why question with an answer such as 'because it is' or even 'because I say so!' will not suffice because such responses are neither logical nor satisfactory in terms of their thinking, and do not do justice to children's capacity to think through what they encounter as they try to make sense of what they find.

Children's questions, puzzles, problems, solutions and fascinations have formed the substance of this chapter demonstrating the active and creative ways in which children learn, how they think about the world and make sense of their experiences of it. The view of children as capable and serious learners and thinkers is a recurring theme throughout this book.

2
SOME QUESTIONS ABOUT SCHEMAS

This chapter is about teachers' (and other professional educators') thinking. When early childhood educators first learn about schemas they often need time to reflect on what this new information means to them. People I have met on numerous courses and conferences which focus on schemas and young children's learning experience a number of emotions: anxiety, concern, excitement, fear and puzzlement to name but a few. These different reactions and emotions reflect the challenge which can be presented by any new-found information. Thinking about newly encountered theories may challenge established practices and threaten the values which have been held, even cherished, for some years. Teachers of children under 5 think deeply about the learning and development of the young children with whom they work and, having pondered, they often ask many questions.

This chapter considers some of the questions which I have heard teachers and other early childhood educators ask about schemas, and offers some personal reflections in response. The following questions are typical examples of those which arise when professional educators begin to think about the implications of theory which suggest that children's thinking can be developed by following their intrinsic forms of thought, their schemas.

In the absence of a large bank of research data to draw upon, the responses to some questions are in the form of personal interpretations which may highlight areas for further research. Where possible, relevant theory and research evidence are used.[1] Such a chapter represents something of a risk. To say 'I think' is to expose what is at the heart of one's actions in working with young children and their parents. Here I am sharing my thinking and my understanding, not because it is definitive but because I believe that it is important that those who are interested in children's learning and development share their thinking and their questions in the hope that a clearer understanding will be reached through professional and pedagogical dialogue.

I hope that this chapter will help to put together a few pieces of the jigsaw puzzle of our understanding of children's thinking. It is written with the intention of making a contribution to the discussion rather than a conclusive statement.

What are schemas?

We are now more knowledgeable about the learning patterns of babies and how they might think and learn. Goldschmied (1989) demonstrates how babies, given safe, stimulating and supportive opportunities, will use their senses to learn about objects they encounter. In so doing they enter into a world of discovery, puzzlement, social encounter and communication. Anyone who watches a young baby will see that some early patterns of behaviour (or schemas) are already evident. As babies suck and grasp, they rehearse the early schematic behaviours which foster their earliest learning. Early patterns of behaviour seen in babies become more complex and more numerous, eventually becoming grouped together so that babies and young children do not perform single isolated behaviours but co-ordinate their actions. Toddlers work hard, collecting a pile of objects in the lap of their carer, walking to and fro, backwards and forwards, bringing one object at a time. They are working on a pattern of behaviour which has a consistent thread running through it. Their patterns of action and behaviour at this point are related to the consistent back-and-forth movement. The early schemas of babies form the basis of the patterns of behaviour which children show between the ages of 2 and 5 years, and these in turn become established foundations for learning.

Athey (1990) maintains that children will notice elements from their surroundings, depending upon their interest at the time, and that they have their own intrinsic motivation which must be facilitated by materials and support from adults. She focused on how 2–5-year-old children also work on particular patterns of behaviour, referring to each of these patterns as a schema and defining a schema as: 'a pattern of repeatable behaviour into which experiences are assimilated and that are gradually co-ordinated' (*ibid.*, p. 37). A number of patterns of behaviour were identified and named by Athey according to their characteristics. For example, the 'vertical schema' is so called because it relates to up-and-down movements. Athey discusses children's learning and development in terms of:

- dynamic vertical
- dynamic back and forth/side to side
- dynamic circular
- going over and under
- going round a boundary
- enveloping and containing space
- going through a boundary.

The actions and marks related to these descriptions of movement can be identified in young children's drawing and markmaking, but Athey illustrates how such patterns can be represented in children's play, their thinking and their language. Athey argues that patterns pervade children's actions and speech as well as their markmaking. Detailed descriptions and discussion on ways in which different patterns of learning can be represented through action, speech and markmaking are given by Athey, who further illustrates in theoretical and practical terms how *forms of thought* (schemas) once identified can be nourished with worthwhile *content*.

If a child is focusing on a particular schema related to roundness, we could say that the child is working on a circular schema. The *form* is 'roundness' and the *content* can be anything which extends this form: wheels, rotating machinery, rolling a ball, the spinning of the planets!

Similarly a child interested on 'up and downness' could be working on a vertical schema. The *form* is 'up and down'; related *content* can include using ladders, using the climbing frame, watching parascending or sky-diving, riding in a lift or on an escalator. In the same way, if a child is interested in enclosing and enveloping schemas, the *form* is 'insideness', and related *content* may include wrapping presents, hatching chick eggs, *en croûte* cookery, mining and burrowing.

Why do some children seem obsessed with one particular activity, repeating it over and over again?

Liam was observed on many occasions putting cups, saucers, plates and other home-corner crockery in the home-corner sink. As soon as he had put all he could find into the sink he walked away and left them. This child might have been interested in spaces which contain and his own ability to put things inside things. He was perhaps seeking out experiences which enabled him to work on different aspects of enclosing and containing. Nursery staff need to make further observations of Liam and, if the pattern is consistent, provide other ways of extending the 'enclosing' schema. Extension activities need to embrace challenging curriculum content so that his thinking is extended. Children who are apparently repeating actions which seem aimless should be observed carefully by staff who can note precisely what children are doing. Staff can try to decide from their observations how valuable children's activities are. New experiences and interventions need to be based on detailed observations underpinned by the educator's knowledge of each child as an individual learner.

What happens to a schema once a child has established it?

Schemas, or repeatable patterns of behaviour, speech, representation and thought can extend learning as they become fitted into children's patterns of thought. Early schemas seem to provide the basis for later learning. Athey (1990) describes how early 'back and forth' schemas can be observed in young children 'toddling and dumping'. Later 'back and forth' actions can be supported and extended with, for example, stories of 'going and coming' (see Chapter 7) or through experiences involving map-reading and map-making. Much more research is needed, but early schemas can connect together to provide the basis for later related experiences which can be assimilated into more complex concepts.

Sixteen-month-old Declan walked back and forth between a pile of toys and his father. Each time he delivered one toy from the pile into his father's lap.

Eventually there were no toys left in the original pile and they were all heaped on the father's lap. Declan experienced several things through this exchange. He was moving between two points: A, the toys, and B, his father. This early backwards and forwards action could lay the foundations for concepts of 'here' and 'there', beginning and ending, starting and finishing, as children move physically and later think about moving between, for example, 'my house' and 'my friend's house', 'my house' and 'my playgroup'. Declan was perhaps also making a social and emotional connection between himself and his father. Declan was giving, his father was receiving. Declan was leaving and returning – his father was always where he left him! Many who work with young children with schemas in mind see connections between children's 'academic' learning and their social and emotional development.

Children can be seen not only making cognitive connections but also making relationships between themselves and others. An 18-month-old girl was waiting in the departure lounge of an airport with her parents. She had her own bag of toys beside her and there were two other carrier bags which contained duty-free purchases, perfume, chocolates and whisky. The little girl began moving between her mother and father, first giving a toy to her mother then retrieving it and walking to her father to offer it to him. The parents played the game, smiling and saying 'thank you' each time they were given a toy, and waving 'bye-bye' each time she left them. The game was then extended to include another passenger, waiting on a seat near the family. This person was offered the toy and followed the 'rules' of the game as they had been demonstrated. The little girl then began delivering a number of toys to the stranger, leaving them on the seat beside her. When she had emptied her own bag of toys, she then began to offer the stranger the contents of the parents' duty-free purchases, smiling at the stranger each time she offered something and looking back at her parents too. This game ended when mother and father stepped in to prevent their perfume and whisky being donated to a complete stranger! This little girl, like Declan, was moving backwards and forwards, testing the power of her own actions, and making a new relationship, a new connection between herself and someone else who, up to now, she had not met. This she could do in the safety of her parents' gaze, to whom she looked from time to time for reassurance and approval.

It is interesting to think about the future of the 'going and coming' patterns of toddlers. Seven-year-old Craig was able to represent his knowledge of space and place and of going and coming by drawing a map of the area around his school (Figure 2.1). It shows the position of the school and the streets which surround it. Some roads are labelled, arrows show the direction to approach the roundabout and buildings are named. Craig explained: 'I know where you go around here because this is where I go with my brother on my bike. To get to my house you go down this road and then turn and go across there.' This 7-year-old's map represents knowledge, connection of ideas and understanding derived from experiences. In terms of pattern, it builds upon early experiences of toddling backwards and

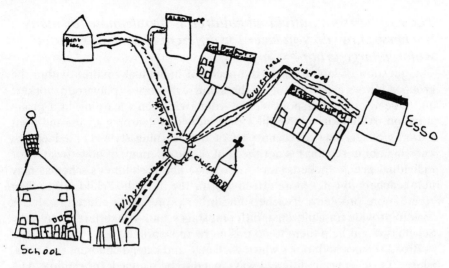

Figure 2.1 Craig's map

forwards, from A to B, and shows again how important are the early behaviours of young children to their learning.

What do you do when you think you have identified a child's schema?

This is a fundamental question. It is not sufficient simply to identify a child's interest: early education needs to challenge children's thinking and extend their learning. When a child appears to be paying attention to a particular pattern, he or she needs to be provided with a range of interesting and stimulating experiences which extend thinking along that particular path. For example: Heather's teacher had noticed that she seemed interested in circular patterns and movement. She planned several 'extension' activities which might 'nourish' Heather's schema:

- A small group of children (including Heather) visited a tyre fitters to watch car tyres being changed.
- Gyroscopes were introduced, adults demonstrated how to use them and children experimented with them.
- Heather's mother took her to the visiting fairground where Heather delighted in several rides down the helter-skelter and on the carousel.

Extensions to children's schemas need to provide opportunities for further learning, for children to talk and for more nourishment for children's fertile minds. Simple extensions for a child's circular schema might include: playing ring games or singing songs (Mort and Morris, 1991) and making collections of circular or round objects. More challenging extensions might draw upon real-life happenings, as in Heather's case, which widen children's experiences of the world and so deepen their knowledge and appreciation of it.

The emphasis on individual children is problematic for many teachers – how do you cater for different children's schemas within a large group?

The question of how to meet the needs of individual children within the group is always a concern of teachers, nursery officers, playgroup workers and indeed anyone responsible for young children's learning in a group situation. All children have their own individual learning styles, and their patterns of learning make up part of this learning style. For educators, knowing about schemas is not the root of the dilemma of how to cater for individual needs. Indeed, more knowledge about children's schemas may help teachers to cater more effectively for the individual child rather than create more problems. Teachers and other professional educators always seek to provide for children at different stages, and with different interests. Schemas might help them to do this more appropriately.

Broad themes and topics which challenge and extend children, and nourish several schemas in different ways, need to be planned. In addition, one-off experiences, small-focus exhibitions and planned opportunities which aim to extend one particular schema for a small number of children, or for an individual, can be incorporated into the curriculum. Working, hands-on exhibitions which match children's schematic interests will attract children who find such things most meaningful to them. Such exhibitions can focus on such themes as packages, wheels, grids and coverings, and are most valuable when they are filled with objects which children can examine, draw and talk about.

When educators have offered a topic to all children, it does not follow that all children have learned the same things from it. All teachers have responsibility for the education of individual children who are grouped together for organisational and financial as well as educational reasons. The match between what teachers teach and what children learn is a key issue which involves observation, planning, teaching, assessment, record-keeping and reflection. These processes are further discussed in Part IV.

Professional educators who have become interested in children's schematic development will know that children will pursue their schemas anyway, whether adults like it or not! Rather than being an additional burden, and something else to worry about, knowledge of schemas can be a useful tool for teachers who work alone, in early entry classes for example. Such knowledge can help with observation, planning, interaction with children, intervention in their work and assessment of their learning. Teachers and nursery nurses working together in nursery schools and classes and other professional educators in day nurseries, playgroups and crèches can, together, create situations which challenge young children, enable 'fine-tuning' of thinking and action, and ensure equality of access and curriculum.

When children play in groups do they choose to play with children who are working on the same schema?

It may be that some children play well together in a sustained and involved way because they 'match' in terms of thought and action. For example, 'house' and 'den' play may well attract children who are interested in ideas of 'inside' and 'outside'. However, many children play co-operatively in groups and perhaps children also play with children whose schematic interests are different but not conflicting.

In a nursery class a group of three children (aged between 3:9 and 4:6), two girls and a boy, were using large hollow bricks to make a 'castle'. The two girls set about the foundations, laying down a square of bricks, one brick high. Both girls worked together, one inside and one outside. At the same time the boy built up the walls, putting more bricks on top of the foundation layer which the girls set out. The girls paid attention to making the doorway and the windows, whilst the boy concerned himself with the height of the walls. Two important ideas were being pursued here. The girls were apparently interested in enclosing and enveloping, and in 'getting in' and 'seeing out'. The boy appeared to be more interested in building towering walls, and the concept of height. As they worked, the three children were engaged in different tasks related to the same project. They discussed questions of 'how big', 'how high', 'how many people can fit in', 'where could the door go', 'how to make the door open and close', 'would there be a letter box'. (They decided there would be no need for a letter box, because in old castles they did not get many letters and if they did someone delivered it on a horse and would knock on the door and ride in!) The three children co-operated, negotiated and worked together purposefully. They worked independently of the teacher who, wisely, allowed this valuable interactive and co-operative exchange to continue uninterrupted, and observed from a distance.

The question of whether schemas can influence children's choice of their partners in play is one which can only be answered with further research. Those who work with young children are in a position to research this for themselves, drawing out instances of co-operative schematic play from their observations of children and making careful analysis of these data. Arnold (1990) worked with parents and colleagues to investigate her notion that children who play together have similar schemas. Nine children were observed during her project, which concluded that the project children all seemed to display repeated patterns of behaviour which were generalisable and that 'On the whole, children tended to play with other children who were interested in doing similar things' (*ibid*., p. 31).

Arnold's study indicated both the difficulties of carrying out such research (even on a small scale) and the value of professional educators doing their own research despite the difficulties. Some children need more than co-ordinated schemas to help them to play together co-operatively, and to be able to negotiate plans and tasks with other children. They need professional educators who are much involved with children's play to encourage co-operation, individual potential and the positive development of children's interests in a climate of mutual discovery, learning and support. This is emphasised in the work of the Froebel Blockplay Project, where Bruce concludes 'Rich blockplay does not just occur. It develops when the adult acts as a powerful catalyst working hard to enable it' (Bruce, 1992, p. 26).

Can a knowledge of schemas help me to change the behaviour of a 3-year-old in the nursery who is persistently throwing objects?

Clearly adults need to intervene when children behave in ways which cause disruption, danger or damage. Obvious questions to ask include: What triggers the behaviour? What happens before? What reaction does it attract? What are the consequences? There are questions to resolve about why children persistently display particular behaviour and whether they may have some yet to be identified difficulty. Educators must observe and aim to intervene before unacceptable behaviour occurs. Identifying children's schematic interest, and providing appropriate activities to match, may help, but it must not be supposed that incorporating knowledge of schemas into practice will solve every problem! Many professional educators use what they know about schemas to divert children from disruptive activities and to focus them on more worthwhile endeavours.

Children who throw in inappropriate contexts may respond to more challenging opportunities for throwing. They may throw to attract attention, to try to gain entry to a group or for other reasons! There may be some form of emotional or behavioural difficulty which needs identification. Finding out 'why' is one issue, tackling the behaviour may well be another. Often the first reaction to a child's throwing is to try to stop him or her. One possibility is to identify the throwing as a way of linking into something which might be important to the child and channel his or her skills and energy more positively. This was the case with Simeon. He was 3 years and 3 months old when he began nursery. His young mother was anxious about his 'temper tantrums' and his bouts of throwing whatever he could find.

Nursery staff observed Simeon carefully and tried to engage his interest in experiences which involved throwing before situations arose which prompted a throwing tantrum. Challenged to find worthwhile curriculum opportunities which involved throwing, the nursery staff became very creative and inventive. Obvious activities such as throwing and catching balls, quoits and bean bags had their place in Simeon's daily experiences but catching was a skill which Simeon was still learning and throwing was something he had perfected to a fine art! Nursery staff were keen that activities which Simeon encountered in nursery were worthwhile learning opportunities for him. He and other children became involved in making targets to throw wet sponges at – the mark left by the sponge was used to identify the score. Sometimes targets had numbers on, other times colours or shapes. Energy and interest were channelled into an activity which absorbed a group of children in a range of learning opportunities and experiences: taking turns; writing 'scores' on large charts; aiming;

co-ordinating body movements; talking; moving; co-operating as a group and sometimes in 'teams'; interacting with peers and adults; and making up new 'rules' for a game. Other throwing activities included: using small balls attached to elastic which returned to the thrower; experimenting with yoyos; and flight-testing paper aeroplanes.

Early-years educators with some knowledge of schemas are in a good position to tackle situations where children's behaviour presents something of a challenge. If children's behaviour becomes a difficulty in terms of its meaning or its management (or both), making detailed observations needs to be part of any course of action. Clearly, young children cannot always be allowed to do exactly as they choose in school or at home. They need clear boundaries. Adults need to explain that certain habits are not acceptable, when they are not in their interests or in the interests of others. Detailed observation of a child who is at first glance creating *disorder* may provide further information to shed light on what is really happening. The child may be *reordering*, acting according to a particular schematic concern.

Children cannot be allowed, in the pursuit of their schemas, to misuse equipment or impede the work of other children. This kind of problem often arises if children are unstimulated and unmotivated by what is available for them to do. Early childhood education must offer a multiplicity of challenging activities and experiences which children can engage in and which foster a number of schemas. Worthwhile curriculum content is that which is broad and balanced and relevant to children's developmental needs. A curriculum needs to be relevant to children and pertinent to individual needs and interests. Such opportunities will lead to motivated children who are absorbed in valuable learning processes.

What place does knowledge of schemas have for teaching children with Special Educational Needs?

The term 'Special Educational Needs' covers such a broad spectrum of learning difficulty that generalisation here is unwise. However, like all teachers, teachers of children with special educational needs should be fully equipped both philosophically and pedagogically. Therefore, knowing about schemas and children's patterns of development means that when teachers observe children they are able more fully to understand and interpret what they see.

Not enough is known of the detailed activity of children across a spectrum of needs and abilities, but there is every reason to suppose that their teachers might identify some particular patterns of behaviour like those discussed in this book – for some of the children they teach.

It seems that everything children do could be called a schema. How useful are schemas really?

When professional educators give labels to children's schemas they are using and developing a professional language to identify consistent patterns of action. What a 'schema' is called is a way of labelling children's consistent patterns of action, and schemas are useful as an observational tool. They provide another way of looking at children, by giving a focus to observational details which might otherwise become a list of disconnected events without much indication of learning or possible action to follow. Identifying a child's activities in terms of different schemas will be only the first part of the process; the next important step is to use detailed observations of children to decide how best to extend their learning. It is the detail of these observations which is important. Compare the two observations below which report the same event:

Observation version 1   Carole was playing in the home corner. She set up the ironing board and did some ironing. Then she washed the cups and saucers and tidied up. She wrote a shopping list and dressed up, took a bag to the 'shop' in the nursery garden.

Observation version 2   Carole was playing *in the home corner*. She pulled the ironing board *across* the entrance and did some ironing. She put the 'ironed' clothes *in* the wicker basket. She collected the *cups* and *saucers* and placed them *in* the *bowl in* the *sink*. She 'washed' them and then put them *in* the *cupboard*. She made some circular marks on a piece of paper, folded it and put it *in an envelope*. She put the envelope *in her pocket*. She put the *purse in her shopping bag* and fastened it shut. Carole *wrapped* a shawl *around* her shoulders and went out into the nursery garden where a tent had been set up as a shop. She went *inside*.

The detail in version 2 gives more information about the form of Carole's thinking than does version 1, which notes that she was involved in aspects of domestic play. Version 2 provides more insights into the schematic nature of Carole's play, showing that she seemed to be exploring *insideness* with a continuity of thinking and consistency of action throughout all she did.

Though little has been written about schemas in the sense used in this book, some LEAs such as Cleveland (Nicholls, 1986) and Sheffield (Sheffield LEA, 1988; 1989; Nutbrown and Swift, 1993) have produced booklets that contain observations of children which illustrate certain schemas. In considering the work of LEAs as well as that of the Froebel Early Education Project (Athey, 1990), it appears that, given schemas as the focus, parents and professional educators are able to observe the fine detail of children's actions and to note the key elements of children's talk that illuminates their thinking and can provide the foundations on which learning can be built. According to Athey (1981, pp. 361–2): 'Systematic behaviour is curiously under-researched in children from two to five years. Behaviours of this stage are often described as idiosyncratic, but schemas of action, when recognised, serve to unite a wide range of apparently different instances of children's activities.'

I feel that the idea of schemas is interesting but how can we share these things with parents? What will their reaction be?

Some teachers feel that they want to know more about theories of child development and learning before they discuss them with parents. Others believe it is important to share new knowledge with parents even though it is still new and incomplete for them. How professional educators respond to this question depends upon the relationships they have with parents, their own depth of knowledge and their confidence in sharing their professionalism. It is important that parents have the opportunity to find out about this way of thinking of children's learning and development, and effective ways of sharing this knowledge are needed. Chapter 10 discusses more fully aspects of working with parents.

How can we use our knowledge of schemas to develop links between home and nursery settings?

When parents, teachers and other early-childhood educators work in partnership to share their observations on the children they live and work with, the possibility of continuity in children's learning and development is increased. Underpinning knowledge of children's development and supporting theories can sometimes shed light on otherwise incomprehensible behaviour. Teachers who have shared their interest in schemas and talked with parents about the ways in which they use this theory to support children's development have often found that parents become more interested in this way of looking at and making sense of children's actions, their talk and their markmaking. Chapter 10 discusses different ways of working with parents so that ideas about schemas can be shared. The following example shows what can happen when teachers share their professional knowledge with parents who then use what they have learned further to help their children and understand their development.

Three-year-old Lulu was absorbed by and interested in circular shapes and motion. She toured the nursery looking for circular shapes, identifying circular objects – bowls, wheels, knobs, turning tap handles. The teacher told Lulu's mother about Lulu's interest, how staff were encouraging her to identify circular shapes and how this would support aspects of her mathematical development. The next morning Lulu and her mother arrived with a carrier bag filled with Lulu's 'circles'. Lulu had collected them together at her house on the previous evening – enlisting the help of her mother and baby brother!

Links between home and nursery, school or playgroup, can be reinforced as parents and professional educators draw on each other's observations of children playing in the home and in their group settings, finding ways of extending children's ideas. Lulu and her mother went with a small group of children and a nursery nurse to visit a working water wheel which developed the concept of roundness and introduced the dynamics of movement and cause-and-effect relationships.

How long do schemas last?

In the absence of longitudinal research to draw upon, it is impossible to answer such a question. But the lack of an answer to this question is not necessarily problematic, however, if teachers use observations to inform their daily work with children. A child will explore a schema for as long as he or she is absorbed by it. His or her pattern of thought needs to be supported by challenging content which will embellish learning and experience. Whilst it seems possible to observe particular and predominant schemas in young children, it appears that schemas connect and combine in older children as they tackle more sophisticated and complex tasks and experiences.

What do you do if a child seems 'stuck' on one schema?

Professional educators become sensitised to the times when children appear to be locked into apparently 'aimless repetition' as well as times when children are repeating actions as a valuable part of their learning process. When children get 'stuck', they are often stuck in terms of schematic 'content'. Ways need to be found to extend the content, while still matching the *form* of a child's thinking, that is to say, the form can be nourished whilst the child is diverted from repetitive *content*. Asif appeared to be interested in a vertical schema. He repeatedly (and loudly) built and demolished brick towers for his super-hero figures to climb and jump from. Positive learning from this activity had been apparently exhausted. It is at this point that teachers need to intervene. If a child seems stuck on a schema – going over and over the same experiences and actions – careful planning and thought needs to be given to providing further learning opportunities. Planned interventions which are also in tune with the child's schemas and which offer the child the opportunity to learn and develop further need to be introduced. This is how nursery staff developed the curriculum for Asif.

The nursery nurse arranged for Asif, with a small group of children and their parents, to visit a local shopping mall and to ride in the glass lift and up and down on the escalator. Play experiences in the nursery reflected this when the children, on return, used the climbing frame to represent the lift and the escalator. Asif's drawings also represented 'the stairs you stand still on' and 'the box that shut you in and lift you up'. Super-heroes were not excluded for long from this added dimension. The children's play soon included people 'stuck' in the lift who needed to be rescued (enter Superman!). Later extensions to this theme included lifting objects with a pulley system using a rope over a branch of a tree. This introduced the children (through hard physical effort and much thought) to problems of power and weight, strength and fastenings, thus fostering ideas related to early scientific discovery.

Can you interrupt a schema?

When professional educators ask this question they are concerned about disrupting the finely balanced process of children's thought. Those who have tried to divert children's attention to activities which do not match their current interests will know that children will not be interrupted in their doing and thinking unless it suits them! Parents who have tried to dissuade babies from throwing toys from their prams or high chairs know the impossibility of diverting children from the activity; indeed, rather than diverting the baby, adults become necessarily involved in their game.

Educators who observe, interact with and intervene in children's play know that sometimes their interventions are well tuned and well timed whilst on other occasions they are not. Teaching young children is not an exact science; we must use the knowledge and skills at our disposal to do the best we can and it seems that schemas can provide a way of teaching 'in tune' with children's cognitive concerns.

Is there an order in which children tend to go through schemas?

More research, with detailed studies of individual children, is needed to answer this question with confidence. It may help to think of some kind of continuum of schematic development where schemas become increasingly co-ordinated. Work on the development of children's early markmaking can help us to speculate about the possible existence of a sequential order of schemas. We can see a clear pattern in the area of children's markmaking development in the work of Rhoda Kellog (Plaskow, 1967), who identifies a sequence of markmaking development in young children. In her sequence, dots, dabs and straight lines precede enclosures and connected marks.

Given that children working on particular patterns of thought can represent their schemas through making marks and talking as well as through their actions, it may follow that 'vertical' and 'back and forth' schemas emerge before 'enclosing and enveloping' schemas. It is probably not as simple as this, though, as children work on the same schematic theme at different stages in their development and incorporate and co-ordinate a number of schemas as they develop.

It may be helpful to think of the notion of 'schemas revisited', where children build up their knowledge through their absorption in particular schemas, move on to explore other schemas and, later, with more maturity of action, language and thought, return to explore a schema further. Detailed longitudinal studies of children at home and in their group settings will provide further insights into the cumulative nature of schemas but at present such insights into children's learning are few.

Reporting on the Froebel Blockplay Project, Gura (1992, p. 65) writes: 'Children often return to forms already mastered, to try out a novel or more complex variant, such as the stacking of vertical enclosures. Sometimes, when it looks as if a particular form has dropped out of the child's repertoire, it reappears in combination with the latest discovery.'

Do all children eventually include all schemas in what they do?

Again, more research into the learning and development of individual
children is needed. What is important is that observations of children at
any point in time lead to the planning of appropriate experiences for them
which match their form of thinking. Certainly in terms of graphic representation, through writing and drawing, they eventually work on numerous
schematic forms. It may, therefore, be reasonable to suppose that this is so
for action and speech as well.

Whilst young children can sometimes be observed paying attention to a
particular schema, older children's learning involves co-ordination of
schemas. *Co-ordination* and *connection* mark important progression in
learning at all stages where combinations and co-ordinations of schemas
develop into higher-order concepts.

Does all, or most, of a child's activity at a particular time fit into a single schema?

In answer to this question I will refer to the children in my own study when
I observed 40 children aged 3–5 years in one nursery class over an academic
year. Several of the children exhibited behaviour which could be related to
a number of schemas. Other children tended to work on a 'dominant'
schema for a while, selecting activities and experiences which fitted into
their current schema, but co-ordination and connection of schemas is part
of human development. The chapters in Part II will provide further details
and examples related to this question.

Is work outside a child's schema counter-productive or fruitless?

No! If the curriculum is based on worthwhile content which draws on real-
life experiences, engages children in talking, listening, experimenting, sol-
ving problems and thinking, it is not fruitless. The point here is that the
'match' needs to be found between what is being learned and what is being
taught. This 'match' may be enhanced if curriculum material is in tune with
children's schematic concerns, identified through observation.

Everything could be attributed to schemas – what about other theories and philosophies?

There are of course many ways of thinking about things and interpreting
children's actions and their learning, and different theories may be useful
at different times. For example, whilst 4-year-old Kerrie played in the sand
she said, 'Bury up the baby – cover her all up.' The teacher interested in her
schema may see this as behaviour relating to an enclosing schema, whilst in
a different context, a psychologist or playtherapist may attribute this behaviour to resentment of her new baby sister. Both interpretations might
need to be examined further. Athey (1990) gives a similar example of Lois
(3:5) who drew her younger brother Jock in his cot, covered her whole

drawing with a blanket (a square of sticky paper) and said, 'I've covered him up with a blanket.' She then said, 'And I'll put the cot in the cupboard [pause] and I'll put the cupboard in a cave.' Athey (*ibid.*, p. 152) remarks that this example could suggest 'sibling rivalry', 'if interpreted within a Freudian framework. However this explanation could not be applied to the dozens of similar examples that were observed around this time, including the wrapped pancake, the darkened house and the "covered over" worm.'

Those who live and work with young children use a whole range of perspectives in order to make judgements about the meanings of the things they say and do; those who include schemas as part of their thinking will do the same. Schematic theory should be used as a flexible and useful tool for teaching and learning, which should work for educators. Educators should not be slaves to theories but sufficiently informed about theories of learning to make use of them in their work.

Adults working with young children use their knowledge of children as individual human beings, and their understanding of theories about child development and learning to make sense of the things children do and say. Using schematic theory in the teaching of young children is a way of using theory to identify, build on and increase children's strengths, interests and capabilities rather than focusing unduly on the things which as yet they cannot achieve.

This chapter has given some indication of the depth of thinking which teachers engage in when they begin to consider the development of the children with whom they work in terms of schematic theory. It shows that the quest to understand children's minds continues and that teachers and other professional educators have a professional interest in understanding children's thinking. The questions upon which this chapter is based came from teachers who spent time developing their own knowledge and thinking. The children they work with are rich indeed, for they are taught by people who ask 'why' as well as 'how', 'what' and 'when'. Nothing can stop children thinking, and young children need to be equipped, and challenged, to *think* as well as to *know*. Teachers and other professional educators cannot teach effectively without professional knowledge about thinking and knowing, they need to think about their work. Knowing about schemas enables them to extend their thinking and develop their practice. Teachers in the field of early childhood who concern themselves with new knowledge and how to apply that knowledge to their practice are well placed to help the next generation of children to grow up as thinkers too, extending children's thinking with worthwhile curriculum content and processes of teaching.

Notes

1. For a detailed consideration of aspects of theory in relation to this topic, see Athey (1990).

Part II
Children's patterns of learning

3

CONSISTENCY, CONTINUITY AND PROGRESSION IN YOUNG CHILDREN'S LEARNING

The notion of consistency in the behaviour and minds of children under 5 years of age might still raise an eyebrow or two, particularly when some adults continue to talk of very young children as being inconsistent, spasmodic and idiosyncratic in their approach to life and learning. Pattern and consistency, however, are features of young children's development which are identifiable when adults take time and patience to look for them. The identification of children's schemas (their patterns of learning) can be used by teachers, parents or other educators to provide learning experiences attuned to their patterns of interest, and therefore provide consistency of learning opportunity. Effective educational provision for young children must have consistency. This consistency can be considered in terms of three 'constants':

- adults and their behaviour
- routines and information
- experiences and materials.

Adults and their behaviour

That children under 3 need their own 'key worker' who is with them for the majority of their time in group care is a concept of continued debate (Rouse, 1990 Goldschmied and Jackson, 1994; Abbott and Moylett, 1997). There are times when children under 5 need the consistency of a particular adult. Children often choose this special 'someone' after forming an initial attachment during a settling-in period. In some cases a worker is allocated to a particular group of children. This kind of consistency is important. Parents want to know with whom they first need to talk about their child when they want to share something or discuss a concern. Children also need to know to which adults they can turn if they want to share an excitement and who will help with what.

Teachers, nursery nurses and other educators and carers in group settings must adopt consistent approaches with children and with their parents. In their daily work with children they provide one of the constants in children's learning lives. Children need to be able to predict how adults might react to certain situations so that they can sometimes take some risks; perhaps some will risk asking questions, trying out new activities or tackling new problems. Children are more likely to 'risk' new things if they have adult support and a sense of how adults will respond to their ventures.

Routines and information

The second 'constant' leads on from that of adults and how they behave. Children need to 'know where they are' to be able to operate with confidence and effectiveness in their nursery or group. If things change, they need their 'constant' of adult support to help them to cope with and learn from the new, sometimes puzzling, frightening and challenging experiences. Children need the security of knowing what will happen and when. They need to have clear explanations if things change and time to adjust to these changes. Information which they can understand is important in helping children to adapt to new situations and to make the most of their daily experiences.

Experiences and materials

The third 'constant' of early education centres on the curriculum provision made for children on a day-to-day basis. There need to be some elements of consistency surrounding those things which children see when they enter the nursery at the start of the session. The experiences that unfold and in which they engage can be accessed more meaningfully when supported with familiarity. Children can get on with the business of learning when they are not encumbered with such worries as where to find things, who to ask or what to do. Children need to know that some things will remain the same each day, for example, that the woodworking bench and necessary materials and tools will always be there for them to use; that there will always be some paint; that those favourite books, or a story read today, will be there again to enjoy tomorrow. They need to know that if they begin something today they will be able to complete or add to it tomorrow, thus developing their own continuity of thought and action.

These three 'constants' help to create a consistency of curriculum which enables young children to be *active* and *independent* learners who:

- tackle new things because they feel safe in doing so, are stimulated to try, and because they know that adults will help if needed;
- plan what they will do when they arrive – for example, deciding 'When I get to nursery this afternoon I'm going to paint some wood and fix it together' or 'I think I might play a game first this morning';

- revisit familiar materials to build on previous experiences such as return-ing to the brick area to build again a structure which was fun to make yesterday.

Knowing that adults, space, time and materials will be 'constant', the same today as yesterday, helps young children to assume more responsibility for what they do and to follow their own consistent threads of thinking and doing without unnecessary hindrance or over-dependence on adults.

The theme of consistency leads us to think about continuity and pro-gression, which are also necessary factors for effective learning. The National Curriculum, first introduced by the Education Reform Act 1988, aimed to ensure a form of continuity and of progression in learning and achievement for children aged 5–16 years and defined how children's learning should progress. In 1996 the publication of what were called 'Desirable Outcomes' for children's learning following nursery education detailed progression of experiences from pre-school through to Key Stage 1. This was a progression in skill and content of some (but by no means all) strands of knowledge. The Report of the Parliamentary Select Committee on Educational Provision for the Under Fives asserted the view of early education as part of an ongoing, continuous process between home and statutory schooling:

> Early education should be seen not as something separate and apart, but rather as the first step on the path into a relevant, coherent and integrated curriculum . . . 'Education is a seamless robe . . . The pre-school experience of three-year-olds and four-year-olds is part of a continuum.' At the same time, nursery education does not, and never can, replace the home, but is an extension of it.
>
> (House of Commons, 1988, para. 2.5)

This view was further endorsed by subsequent government documents (Her Majesty's Inspectorate (DES, 1989a) and the Rumbold Committee (DES, 1990a)):

> The best work with under-fives has always taken account of the need for continuity with the teaching and learning which takes place in the next stage of their education. The new legislation (ERA 1988) adds considerable importance to ensuring that full account is taken of the need to promote curricular continuity and progression.
>
> (DES, 1989a, para. 73)

> The wide range of developmental stages and needs of very young children puts a great responsibility on educators to provide a curricu-lum which can take into account the similarities and differences within any group of under-fives and also provide continuity with what went before and progression to what will follow.
>
> (DES, 1990a, para. 63)

Interest in the continuity of learning well precedes the publication of official descriptors of children's learning before five. Athey (1990) described the con-tinuities of children's learning in terms of these 'persistent concerns' and dem-onstrated high-level thinking in areas of the mathematical and the scientific as children pursued their own themes and tackled self-selected problems.

Issues of continuity and progression linking previous, present and future experiences, and their significance for the curriculum for children under 5, need careful consideration. There needs to be clear understanding of what is meant by 'continuity' and 'progression', and of the ways in which early education might achieve continuity and progression for young children's learning and development. Concepts of continuity and progression are more complex than the tomes of government decriptors in the last ten years might suggest. Let us consider, briefly, some of the issues.

First, are we considering continuity of thought as well as action? Are we paying attention to and providing for continuities of children's *ideas* and *interests* as well as continuity of the things they do? Are we considering continuity of *processes* as well as *content*? Are the *products* of early educational experiences overemphasised at the expense of the experiences themselves which might yield no immediate, visible products?

Different facets of continuity and progression need to be considered:

- externally imposed continuity and progression
- teacher-imposed (or teacher-controlled) continuity
- child constructed continuity
- progression in thought
- making meaningful continuities.

Externally imposed continuity and progression

The Education Reform Act 1988 marked the beginning of external and nationally imposed curriculum for children from 5 years onwards – the first era of external continuity and progression for primary-aged pupils. These curriculum continuities were in the form of ten subjects: English, Mathematics, Science, Geography, History, Music, Physical Education, Art, Craft, Design and Technology and (locally agreed) Religious Studies. Since the introduction of the National Curriculum, revisions and the Dearing Review (DfEE, 1997) have resulted in a 'streamlining' of the primary curiculum with emphasis on the 'core' subjects of English, Mathematics and Science. The National Literacy Strategy (DfEE, 1998) brought with it the 'Literacy Hour' to be closely followed by the 'Numeracy Hour' which forced changes in content of literacy and numeracy lessons nationally and ushered in a new era of externally, government-imposed continuity and progression of curriculum provision.

In 1996 the first externally imposed indicators of 'desired' achievements of children as a result of (some form of) pre-school education were published. These focused on literacy, mathematics, knowledge and understanding about the world, and personal and social education (DfEE, 1996).

These indicators set the trend for revision of the curriculum in nurseries, and teachers began to 'adjust' their planning and assessment in order to 'take account of' the so-called 'Desirable Outcomes'. The narrowness of these 'outcomes' of pre-school education might have threatened challeng-

ing forms of nursery curriculum where children pursued their own continuities of thought. These externally imposed influences on pre-school
curriculum and on practices of nursery education were also to herald the
first externally imposed assessment of children from September 1998
(SCAA, 1997). It would remain to be seen how external impositions of
curricular content and of assessment might influence the development and
effectiveness of educational provision for children in the pre-statutory
period.

Teacher-imposed (or teacher-controlled) continuity

This view of continuity could require (or suppose) that children can focus
on a theme over some weeks. Whilst an initial idea for the theme might be
derived from a child's idea or experience, it is usually nursery teachers,
leading a team, who plan and extend further content of the theme. The
cross-curricular nature of the thematic approach to teaching young children is intended to contribute to the all-round learning opportunities and
to a 'broad, balanced, relevant and differentiated' curriculum (DES,
1989a). Thematic approaches to curriculum planning and organisation can
be a way of ensuring curriculum balance and breadth, and a way of inte-
grating elements of learning rather than falsely compartmentalising them
into subjects. However, experience suggests that continuity in terms of a
theme lasting a number of weeks is typically imposed by nursery staff,
offered to the children, and is content-based. For example, a theme on
journeys and journeying can focus on elements of this topic that touch on
all the nine areas of learning and experience advocated by HMI (DES,
1989a) and the Rumbold Committee (DES, 1990a) to provide a broad and
balanced curriculum: 'The aesthetic and creative, the human and social, the
linguistic and literary, the mathematical, the moral, the physical, the scientific, the spiritual and the technological' (DES, 1989a, para. 20).

Since 1996 the desirable outcomes have required that teachers and other
pre-school educators demonstrate how their planning 'delivers' or 'covers'
the outcomes. This could have the effect of limiting curriculum to what is
required and those who work with young children must be constantly
vigilant that the continuity they control is also that which challenges appropriately children's thinking.

A topic on journeys and journeying for example, could include: early
mapwork; related stories told and read; considerations of forms of trans-
port and ways of getting to different places; how different modes of travel
work; forms of energy; historic journeys and so on. Early-years educators
will be familiar with this method of constructing a broad and balanced
curriculum, as they are with the need to relate such planning to official
requirements of the day. Such planning can embrace a holistic view of the
curriculum, set learning in real and realistic contexts and has the potential
to resist the compartmentalisation of particular sets of ideas, rather inte-
grating them into a coherent whole. This type of planning also draws upon

children's interests and can be a way of making learning opportunities dynamic and worthwhile. But this is only the *offered* curriculum, so teachers and other educators who claim to offer high-quality educational provision need to find out the extent to which each child has *received* and made use of and learned from that which is offered.

The type of continuity across the curriculum achieved through thematic work can be a useful planning tool. However, *teacher-constructed continuity* is not necessarily the kind of continuity that fulfils children's need for continuity in their learning and thinking, and teacher-constructed continuity which is informed *only* by external constructions of continuity is unlikely to contain the responsive opportunities for learning and thinking to which many young children readily respond. Observations of children thoroughly absorbed in their work as part of the curriculum offered to them are needed to find out how much the children have gained and learned from it. Watching children, and listening to children, are essential to understanding their learning. Mary Jane Drummond (1993, p. 59) wrote: 'Our attempts as teachers to get inside children's heads, and understand their understandings, are enriched to the extent that children themselves are prepared to give us, through their talk, access to their thinking.'

Child-constructed continuity

Children's schemas, identified and nurtured, can provide opportunities for continuity in learning. Children's persistent threads of action and thought seem to be fundamental elements which link what children do and think with the process of learning and with its content. This kind of continuity, that which children create in the process of exploring, thinking and learning, belongs at the heart of any discussion of curriculum continuity. Viewed in this way, schemas can be considered at the core of children's developing minds.

Some continuities constructed by individual children may be identified as threads of thinking (or schema) which 'connect' different areas of content. Without observation and reflection on the part of professional educators, these fine threads remain invisible and children's chosen activities may appear to lack continuity either of content or of thought. When individual patterns of action and thought are not observed and identified children might be said to be *inconsistent*, to lack *concentration* and to be unable to choose for themselves, let alone take any responsibility for their own learning. Young children are often described as 'flitting' from one activity to another. However, when professionally informed educators look closely at what children are doing in each apparently unconnected activity they sometimes find (and understand) important cognitive links; such cognitive connections remain invisible to those who are uninformed and lack an underpinning knowledge of the theories of children's learning. For example: a 3-year-old spends his time moving from one activity to another. First he digs in the sand; he moves on to make a cup from some clay; then he goes outside to 'hide' under the branches of a willow tree; next he paints – two ovals on a large sheet of paper with a dab in the centre of each. 'Mices in cages,' he says. Considered from the point of view of *discontinuities of action*, he moves in about six minutes between four different activities – sand, clay, willow tree, paint. Considered in terms of *continuity of thought* he creates: *a hole* (in the sand), and *a container* (in the clay), he *hides* in an *enveloping space* (under the willow tree), and he represents two mice *enclosed* in cages (using paint). Reflected upon in this way, the links or *continuities* in his behaviour become apparent and can be described as part of his enveloping/enclosing schema, his predominant cognitive concern.

When children's actions are observed with schemas (rather than simply content) in mind, it becomes possible to interpret children's approaches to learning differently. It is through schemas, and the fitting of content to different schematic threads, that children's own constructions of reality can sometimes be identified and subsequent opportunities for further continuity in learning created. Looking at learning in this way can be a little like unlocking a door, shining a light on previously darkened areas, seeing anew.

Four-year-old Vicky irritated her parents when she persistently removed tea towels from the kitchen to wrap her teddies in and put them to bed. When participating in a discussion about children's schema held at Vicky's nursery, her mother realised that it was not just the teddies who were being used in this wrapping-up behaviour. Vicky always carried a bag with her when she went out. In the bag there was often a smaller bag and then several other bags and purses filled with small toys, coins, a hanky, note-paper, indeed seemingly whatever would fit! Vicky's mum had always ac-cepted this behaviour as Vicky 'being a little girl' and wanting to be like her mum (taking a variety of useful things in her handbag). Vicky might well have been modelling her mother to some extent, but what underpinned this and other related examples of similar behaviour can be identified as the schematic thread of consistency in her behaviour. This child was paying attention in a concentrated and systematic way to *insideness*. When Vicky's previously irritating behaviour was interpreted in this new way, (a way that suggested that she was exploring and learning and engaged in an important kind of thinking), Vicky's mother decided that she would make small 'teddy-bear sheets' out of an old sheet and enable Vicky to continue her wrapping behaviour whilst keeping track of her tea towels.

Progression in thought

The gradual evolution of schemas, and the extension of early forms of chil-dren's thought, can eventually lead to connections between schemas and therefore to the formation of new ideas. One example of progression in thought can be seen in a child's gradual development in drawing the figure of a person. Initial representations may be simple vertical lines later followed by oval representations. Later some marks may appear inside or outside the oval that represent parts of the face; finally the oval core becomes attached to vertical and horizontal lines, and the whole represents a body with arms and legs. Over a period of two or three years (sometimes less, sometimes more) the drawing of a human figure develops in this way. An area for further research lies in the possible links between children's representations and their emotional development. Children first represent themselves and their own viewpoint, their egocentric view of life, and later become more aware of themselves in the world and themselves in relation to others (Matthews, 1994). The development of core and radial drawings may also link with the time when children begin to make social and emotional connections with their peers and others. Other figures appear in their drawings, seemingly at the time when children become aware of themselves and others: their brother, sister, mum, grandad, their dog, cat or goldfish.

So how does the early content of children's persistent puzzling and thought lead to progress or development? The content of young children's thought arising from an enveloping/enclosing schema might relate to the idea of hiding or covering up or 'being inside'. When these fundamental ideas develop, children will begin to understand ideas related to capacity or surface area. Later still children start using symbols to represent capacity, in the same way as adults understand that the petrol indication light on the dashboard of a car represents how much fuel is in the tank, or that the dipstick indicates the level of oil in the reservoir. Children who understand about 'inside' and 'outside' and about increasing and decreasing size will find the story of *The Secret in the Matchbox* (Willis, 1991) – where a young boy keeps a tiny dragon in a matchbox, but when the box is opened the dragon grows and grows – both understandable and amusing.

Making meaningful continuities

Continuity is an essential element of quality in any early education curriculum. To be effective, the curriculum content offered to children must find a match in the content of their thinking and with their capabilities. Bruce (1987, p. 25) reminds us that 'what children can do (rather than what they cannot do) is the starting point in the child's education'. Some continuity and progression of learning can be achieved in this way by building on children's capabilities.

Difficult though it is to juggle externally imposed requirements with children's needs to construct their *own* continuity, teachers and other early-education professionals need to find ways to provide for continuity which link children's ideas and children's interests with curriculum content. The progression of skills, and the introduction of new materials and content, should support progression of children's thoughts and ideas. These multiple elements are needed. But where skills and prescribed content dominate the curriculum it can be at the expense of other important factors in the continuity of learning. Where skills dominate there is a risk that balance can be lost and that the growth of independent and creative thinkers is limited. Continuity and progression in children's learning can best be achieved if the children – as people and as learners – are respected as *central to* and *active in* the learning process in which they are engaged. Learning opportunities must be meaningful and motivating to children. Continuity of curriculum and progression in learning are best achieved when meaning and motivation are high on teachers' agendas.

Making learning meaningful has been a central focus of the work of those many respected educators who laid the foundations of early child-hood education as it is known today. Reflecting on the work of Froebel, Montessori and Steiner, Bruce (1987, p. 26) wrote: 'Through careful obser-vation, based on knowledge of the stages of child development, the adult can work with the child rather than against what is natural.' In this way, children are more likely to sustain their effort, to struggle and persevere when they inevitably encounter learning which they find difficult.

The Russian psychologist Vygotsky made a significant contribution to theory on children's thinking. He saw learning as a profoundly social pro-cess which needed dialogue and mediation. The clear and crucial role for adults in developing young children's thinking was highlighted through Vygotsky's work. Early-childhood educators today have an awesome task, for the evidence is that they can make a profound difference to the enhan-cement of young children's quality of thought through the experiences they provide and their interactive experiences *with* children.

According to Vygotsky every piece of learning has a history, a base on which it was built, beginning before formal education and based in real-life experiences. When we stop to think of formal learning of say, writing, we can often trace early beginnings well before organised learning (e.g. Good-man, 1980). Early and informal learning occurs when children spend time with adults, working on real situations such as baking, filling the washing machine, gardening, and writing birthday cards. Vygotsky regarded the match between a child's learning and his or her developmental level as all important. He suggested that children had two developmental levels, their *actual* developmental level, what they could actually do independently, and a higher level, that which they may *next* be able to do. Vygotsky identified the interchange between these two levels as the 'zone of proximal develop-ment', the difference between what children can do alone and what they can do with help, support and guidance. He argues 'what a child can do with assistance today she will be able to do by herself tomorrow' (Vygotsky, 1978, p. 87). This notion emphasises the important role of the adult in fostering progression in children's thinking: helping children to move forward in, and develop their ideas through, positive and interactive learning encounters between children and adults.

One of the clearest ways to understand progression in children's learning is to look at individual children over a period of time, observing their schematic interests, seeing how these relate to the development of their behaviour, their speech and their thinking. The next chapter consists of case studies of three children, Gary, Jeanette and Stuart, who are pursuing three different schemas.

4
SCHEMAS AS CONSISTENT PATTERNS OF BEHAVIOUR – STUDIES OF THREE CHILDREN

Introduction

In this chapter the learning experiences of three children, Gary, Jeanette and Stuart, are presented and discussed. Three short case studies use observations of the children's daily work, play and development in their nursery environment and illuminate different elements of continuity and progression in their thinking. By focusing on individual children we can begin to identify ways in which theory about patterns of development (schemas) might be useful in teaching young children.

In looking at Gary, Jeanette and Stuart we can consider three of the schemas identified by Athey (1990): dynamic vertical, containing/ enveloping and dynamic circular. Using the experiences of these children as examples, we can see how children meet and use opportunities for further learning through the exploration of their schemas. In these examples there is visible consistency of forms of thought (the schemas) and a variety of related content of thought (curriculum and life experiences) (Athey, 1990).

Observations of them were made over three terms whilst the children attended a nursery class. All three children showed continuities in their actions that can be analysed to suggest consistent patterns of thinking, as well as continuity and progression in their learning. Whilst what could be called a *dominant* schema is discussed for each child, this does not mean other schemas were not part of the children's repertoires. In each case, all observations of the children were analysed and the schema occurring most frequently for each child is discussed here in detail, illustrating each child's related learning. Once a dominant schema was identified, staff could plan learning opportunities to match the child's concerns and interest.

This chapter illustrates consistent patterns that seem to run through the whole of children's behaviour: their actions, their language, their drawings and their thinking. In discussing the schemas of Gary, Jeanette and Stuart, we will see how speech, graphic communication and actions seem to fit together to form a cohesive pattern.

Examples given here draw on original data from my study of 40 children. The temptation to draw comparisons between these and observations from other publications has been resisted. But others have detailed examples of children's schemas which resonate with those described here (Whalley, 1995; Meade and Cubey, 1995; Sheffield, 1990). What is needed is a 'bank' of information that will help professional educators identify, discuss and thus extend children's learning from a schematic base. This is similar to the call by Stenhouse (1975) for multiple cases that can be drawn upon in the search for commonalities. Different authors have taken different approaches in the search for schemas, but many will recognise the patterns of action, speech, representation and thought illuminated by Athey (1990).

Gary: Dynamic vertical schema

Gary attended the nursery full time for a term before he transferred to the infant school. He had recently moved into the area and had previously attended another nursery in the same local authority. He lived with his mother and younger, 2-year-old, brother in a two-bedroom terraced council house that was just a few minutes' walk away from the nursery.

Gary's markmaking, his movement, the things he constructed and his use of language seemed connected by his interest in things vertical. The following observations show a thread of thinking and doing which seemed to run throughout his work.

Gary (4:7) frequently used the climbing frame in the nursery garden. He climbed to the top, using various routes and usually descended by way of the slide. Gary also used his body to extend and explore height when jumping, bouncing and climbing tree logs, often launching himself into the air with the cry and gestures of the current television super-hero! The experience of climbing higher and dropping down is important for the development of ideas related to increasing and decreasing height and for children to gain a sense of control of their bodies. If children experience such dimensions with their bodies they are better equipped to understand them in the abstract and to represent height and different levels in their drawings and through talk. If children have frequency, variety and richness of experiences they are better equipped to create abstractions from their experiences.

Gary (4:7) painted a series of pictures that included ladders. Figure 4.1 represents 'That's a ladder, that's a man who's gonna climb up it, and that's the sun.' Whilst Gary's drawings were clear and apparently uncomplicated he was able to produce a set of marks that enabled him to portray most things. He could draw straight lines, dots, arcs and circles. He could connect these marks, he could place marks inside other marks and add marks to the outside of others. His use of the grid to represent 'a ladder' matches his interest in climbing up and down. He described the ladders in his drawings as 'useful, 'cos it helps you to go up'. Positioning also seemed

Figure 4.1 'That's a ladder . . .'

important in Gary's drawings. There was always something at the bottom of the ladder, for example the ground, himself, another person or a car, and the sun or a bird was often featured at the top of the ladder.

Playing with the doll's house (4:8) Gary walked some small figures up the stairs saying, 'They need to go up the stairs. They sleep at the top.' Later his play involved people working on the roof of the doll's house. 'They're working up high. They climb up the ladder to fix the slates.'

Understanding and appreciation of gender issues and equal opportunities mean that nursery staff encourage children to use the whole range of equipment and experiences. In this example, Gary demonstrated his interest and competence whilst using the doll's house to create a story that fitted his schematic concerns. Constraints of gender stereotype that reduce children's access to various learning opportunities were not apparent here. The doll's house provided the opportunity to play in a creative and representative way with his earlier real-life experience of seeing the roofers repair damaged roof tiles.

A conversation with Gary's mother revealed that he had been 'helping' some workers who arrived during the school holidays to replace roof tiles. She commented that he would not be distracted from watching them, seemingly fascinated that they were walking on the roof. At the time, he commented, 'They're up a lot, aren't they, mum?'

Gary's mother recalled her amusement with the way Gary expressed his observation that the men were up high, and told him that the men were 'up high'. It is noteworthy that Gary then used the word *high* when he was playing with the doll's house. Children are more likely to assimilate language used by adults when what they say matches children's interests. Words that are out of context or not in harmony with children's current schematic concerns and interests are less likely to be meaningful for children.

Continuing to pursue his interest in vertical movement, Gary (4:8) used the small ladder in the nursery garden and placed it against the wall. He asked if he could 'paint the wall'. This was not encouraged in its entirety (the prospect of Gary and 38 other children with brushes and gallons of paint needs no explanation). Instead, the teacher found a way to satisfy this request. She gave him a large bucket of water and a large brush and suggested that he pretended to paint the wall. Gary was happy with this and began to 'paint' the outside wall. Other children joined him, and he explained the technique: 'I have to climb up four steps first, you do up high first, then you come down lower to do the bottom bits. I saw them do it outside my house.' Gary paid attention to the brickwork he was 'painting' with water. He counted the bricks he had painted and commented that he had 'half the water left' in his bucket. He was able to combine ideas of space and number, achieving some continuity of thought and connection between different ideas.

There had been decorators working on the estate recently, redecorating the outsides of some houses. Again this experience matched Gary's current interest and he represented it in his play. Nursery staff supported and extended Gary's interests, providing the materials he needed in response to his requests, and drawing on their own observations of Gary. Such methods of working served to enhance Gary's learning opportunities.

Gary (4:9) drew a vehicle (Figure 4.2) and said, 'I did a car and it was going really fast and it's got one wheel that's pumped down so it stopped.' He pointed to the smaller wheel in the drawing to indicate which wheel he was referring to. It seems that Gary had found a way to represent his schema through drawing on the experience of riding in his uncle's car when

Figure 4.2 'I did a car . . .'

it had a puncture. The opportunity to see the deflated tyre, the jacked-up car and the process involved in making the car mobile again provided 'food for thought' for Gary and matched his current schema.

When talking about this drawing with Gary, his teacher told him that when a tyre was 'pumped down' it was called 'deflated'. She explained that the tyre in Gary's picture was deflated because it had a hole in it which was called a 'puncture'. Gary seemed to like these words and soon introduced a

game where he pretended that all the bikes in the nursery garden were in
need of repair because they all had punctures.

The ladders in Gary's drawings and his understanding of 'upness' and
'downness' seemed to be a development of his vertical schema. Later
drawings often included a grid or cross of some kind. He filled in spaces using
vertical and horizontal lines and made a series of drawings that included
numerous crosses. This combination of vertical and horizontal marks and
movements seemed to herald the arrival of more complex thinking for Gary.

Gary (4:10) was looking at pictures of spiders' webs in a book, then he
saw a photograph of a child drawing around his hand. Gary spent some
time staring hard at the palms of his hands and tracing the lines on them
with his finger. Later he drew around his hand and filled the outline with a
grid pattern (Figure 4.3). After drawing this he said, 'It's spiders' webs all
over my hand. I saw them in a book.' Gary had seen the match between the
crossed lines in a spiders' web and the crossed lines that naturally occur on
the skin of the palm. This illustrates the potential source and richness of
stimulating material in books when combined with the child's own patterns
of thinking, markmaking and language.

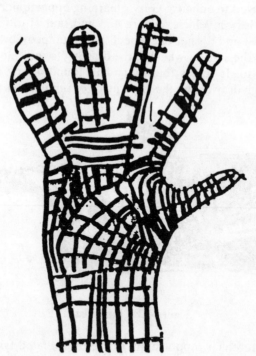

Figure 4.3   'It's spiders' webs all over my hand'

Gary refined his 'line and grid' patterns to the point where he could draw
sophisticated representations of the palm of his hand. Gentle (1985, p. 40)
observed that a child's markmaking evolves according to a 'repertoire of

marks, schemata and observations already made'. Matthews wrote of a collection of Ben's (age 3:3) drawings:

> Changes of states and changes of position seem to be the deep structures – the different aspects of schemas – underlying much of Ben's drawing at this time . . .
>
> (Matthews, 1994, p. 82)

Gary (4:10) utilised much of the nursery equipment and appeared to extend his schema spontaneously. He subsequently represented his experiences. On one occasion, he used a number of large foam cubes to build a tower, saying, 'This is the tall fire tower that goes up higher than you can get.' Then with his friend they played a game of fighting the fire with hoses and used wooden boxes as the crane to reach the top of the tower. Eventually (after a helpful push) with dramatic sound-effects the tower crashed to the floor. Again Gary explained: 'They built it too high. You can't put fires out in scry [*sic*] scrapers, the water won't go up there.'

When the teacher talked with Gary and his friend about their burning skyscraper, Gary explained in some graphic detail about the film he had seen on television in which a fire broke out in a high tower. He described the elevator that travelled up the outside of the building; the raised platforms that would not reach the top because the building was too high; ropes being used to provide a method of escape; and torrents of water pouring from the top of the building. The film had clearly had some profound effect on Gary and he recalled clear details for use in his dramatic play. The amount of vertically related content that this 4-year-old had assimilated was substantial.

There are lessons to be learned from this example. Television, as many will agree, can have a powerful influence on young children. They can pay attention to and retain elements of detail about the images (be they positive or negative) which they see. This book is not about the virtues or dangers of television for children, but we can heed a message. Whilst there is a need to protect children from images that may be disturbing, it can also be possible to use appropriate media opportunities to enhance curriculum opportunities. Curriculum content (to be discussed more fully in Part III) must be drawn from the real world but will also include support material such as video and CD-ROM material. Children need first-hand experiences, such as visits to local places to see, for example, machinery, animals, the fire station, and to enjoy and learn from events such as dance festivals, art and sculpture exhibitions. All these things can be important elements of a worthwhile curriculum and such experiences need frequently to be built into the curriculum for children under 5. This may be familiar to many early-childhood educators, but for so many the familiarity lies in the content of visits rather than the forms of thought that they might inform, nourish and extend.

Gary's interest in firefighting apparently matched the present *form* of his thinking, his schema. Powerful film images captured his imagination: falling debris, cascading water, elevators moving up and down the building, people abseiling on ropes from a great height. The drama in this example cannot be ignored, but it is useful to focus in on the *structures* of thinking which made Gary represent this scenario in his play. Was it pure drama or was it also that so much of the content nourished his vertical schema? Those working with young children need to consider *forms* of thinking when they plan educational visits as part of a topic or theme. A visit to the fire station can nourish a number of schemas and ideas, serving a number of interests, especially when the *forms of thought* (or schemas) are identified and where the *content* is worthwhile and informative. Children interested in ladders may be focusing on the structure rather than the content 'ladder'. So the job of the teacher is not necessarily to focus on *ladders* but to work with the child to explore the question, 'What other things can be used to increase height and facilitate movements from one level to another?'

Jeanette: Containing and enveloping schemas

Jeanette began to attend nursery when she was 3 years and 9 months old. She needed about four weeks to settle happily, during which time her mother and grandmother spent time in the nursery with her each morning. Jeanette lived in a semi-detached council house on the estate in which the nursery was situated. She lived with her mother, father, two older brothers (12 and 14 years) and younger sister who was 6 months old. Jeanette spent much time with her grandmother whilst her mother worked part-time in the local chipshop.

Jeanette made full use of the nursery environment and seemed very imaginative in her play. Many observations of Jeanette in the nursery suggested that containing and enveloping actions underpinned her play, and as would be expected, some observations pointed to other schematic concerns. Where children are engaged in a range of experiences and making use of things they encounter by chance, they develop their thinking, knowledge and understanding about the world. Much of Jeanette's language reflected the underpinning structures of her thinking and helped staff to identify her interests.

Brown (1973) wrote that speech representations which relate to enclosing and enveloping begin at about 2 years old. Piaget and Inhelder (1956) described three types of enclosure: one-, two- and three-dimensional. Jeanette put herself inside enclosures many, many times. She sorted through the dressing-up clothes and then enclosed herself behind the trolley on which they hung. She used the hanging clothes as curtains. She seemed intent upon hiding or being covered up. 'This is my house, come in,' she said, indicating that she had used the dressing-up trolley and clothes to make a house and this was the content of her schema.

This type of play continued when Jeanette climbed inside a climbing frame that formed an enclosed and defined space. Again her language matched her actions: 'This is my little house, I'm in bed.' There were two references to enclosures in this remark, *house* and *bed*. In this sentence, having described her actions, Jeanette added content to her schema: 'I'm in bed.' What she *said* and what she *did* corresponded, showing co-ordination between her speech and her actions.

There were many times when Jeanette, playing in the home corner, blocked off the entrance with furniture: an ironing board, a chair or a piece of fabric fastened between cupboard units. Indeed, she used whatever she could find to bridge the open gap so that she was completely enclosed within the house. Often, when doing this, she would say something like, 'I'm inside now', or 'The door is closed now.' Jeanette seemed to have a need to be entirely enclosed, so sealing the entrance was an important part of her play.

Staff observations were used to identify Jeanette's patterns of thinking which seemed to link her actions and language. The role of early education is not simply to *recognise* children's patterns of behaviour and learning and to *understand* their actions. Teachers must also find ways of *extending* children's thinking and learning, basing their decisions on children's needs as ascertained by careful and detailed observations; their knowledge of child development; and of continuity and progression of learning strands. Teachers of young children develop ways of matching the curriculum they plan to the current interests and concerns of the children with whom they work. Such teachers are inventive, ingenious and imaginative in their work. They involve themselves and intervene in children's play, as appropriate, to extend and challenge their thinking and their doing.

Such was the dexterity of Jeanette's teacher, who used the opportunity of a sudden and heavy snowfall to create dynamic opportunities for learning. A group of children, including Jeanette (4:1), was playing outside in the snow. The teacher watched Jeanette and other children playing with the buckets and spades, digging, moulding, throwing and sliding on the snow. She wondered if she could, or should, channel Jeanette's enjoyment of the snow and help her to work with other children and engage in further experiences of 'insideness'. Knowing that the children would either eagerly accept or resolutely ignore her idea, the teacher suggested that they might try to build a house of snow. The children agreed. They moulded the snow, talked about it, rolled it into small balls and added more snow to make the balls larger. Jeanette jumped into mounds of snow, pretending to hide and a spontaneous and joyful game of 'snow hide-and-seek' followed. Children piled snow into a heap to make a wall, then Jeanette, knowing that her house was made of bricks, organised a number of children to make some bricks out of snow. This was a rather ambitious undertaking, but two passing parents (perhaps envious of their children's snow games) were happy to stop and join in! A retired gentleman who lived opposite the school had been watching from his window. He came to offer his garden spade and the nursery nurse donated her car snow-shovel to the effort. The addition of these tools made construction work easier. The teacher prompted talk about the size and weight of the bricks, and how wide the wall should be. Jeanette was most concerned about how big the 'inside' would be so that everyone could fit inside.

Through this dynamic and co-operative experience, Jeanette's interest here seemed to have moved from simply *being inside* to thinking about the purpose of space, and the importance of size. She was concerned that there should be a roof 'to keep the people dry'. When offered a blanket (used as a tent in the summer) she said that it would 'still let the rain through to the inside' and chose instead to use plastic sheeting supported by a plank of wood. She explained the reasoning for her choice: 'My dad put that on the window when it broke and the rain won't go through this stuff.'

The house building complete, the children shared some warming soup that had been prepared indoors by another group of children working with the nursery nurse. Jeanette remarked that children needed to 'go in and out because they can't all fit in together', and suggested that some of the children who made the soup should sit inside the house. 'They helped us to get warm inside our tummies so they can play in the house too.'

This experience was a balanced episode of sharing and co-operating, involving children, staff, parents and neighbours. There were opportunities to learn about working together and communicating effectively, about physical effort and the need for good tools and warm, waterproof clothing. Children talked about many mathematically rooted aspects: how big, how many, too heavy, too small, just right, will it fit. They discussed angles, corners, shape and position. They talked about their experiences that morning, as they encountered them: the properties of the snow, whiteness, coldness, its melting, the noises on the streets and in the garden, how the snow might change if the sun shone or if the temperature dropped even further. These early scientific notions were a natural part of the chatter of this busy and tenacious group. The teacher made the most of opportunities to maximise individual children's interests and to help them to develop and appreciate different things: working with others, considering size, sharing the digging tools, estimating and measuring spaces.

Clearly the children involved in this rich outdoor experience had meaningful opportunities to talk and learn. Their work was stimulated and extended by a teacher who was tuned into children's interests and skilled at motivating children to work purposefully and co-operatively. These children were learning about working together as well as gaining worthwhile cognitive experience. They were sharing their ideas, their plans and their pleasures as they played with peers and adults to make the snow house. The spontaneous experience of building the snow house fitted well with the planned event of making soup. The teacher and nursery nurse skilfully dovetailed these two activities, making it possible for children and parents to share together in the outcomes of their morning's work.

Markmaking can also provide a clear indication of children's interests. Jeanette represented the movements and actions of containing and enveloping by making marks on paper that matched her motor-level actions of being inside and of placing objects inside containers. From a range of geometric designs printed on paper, Jeanette selected a page printed with divided, concentric circles. Using a wax crayon, she covered the whole area with one colour. Explaining her work, she said, 'I've covered up all the pattern – it's hidden.' The first impression of this apparent scribble could be disregarded as 'careless' or 'thoughtless', but Jeanette's commentary on her work indicated a purpose to her colouring.

The notion of 'being inside' and the enclosure marks Jeanette made were combined when Jeanette gave a verbal account of one of her drawings: 'It's rain, and that's the umbrella, those are the metal things and that's the material that covers over and that's the spider. It's inside the sink, that's the sink.' In this example, Jeanette drew and described objects she knew were coverings or containers, her vocabulary reflecting this interest. Gardner (1980, p. 26) observes that pre-school children generate 'fixed patterns' or 'schemas' for familiar objects in their world. These include a circle radiating lines that typifies the sun. Jeanette used this core and radial (Athey, 1990) to represent spider and umbrella. Gardner (1980) suggests that these basic schemas, once established, can be assimilated into more organised and complex representations of children's experiences. Jeanette drew the objects within her experience to make an illustration of things that were covered or coverings, were contained or containers.

She described three drawings as 'Me *covered up*'; 'Snowman, snow *all around*'; 'A car *covered in* snow', apparently picking out those things from her experience which matched her current schematic interests. The words she used to describe her drawings also showed a connection to ideas of covering and enveloping. Other drawings also suggested links with her containing/enveloping schema. Gardner (1980, p. 11) suggested that children often make their drawings which explore one particular schema in sets of three, four or five. Jeanette made a series of marks on the same day that were all types of enclosure or coverings naming each differently, ascribing content to each:

- a tree, 'a big big tree'
- a snail
- a head
- a sock
- a snake

Jeanette put layer upon layer of paint on a page covering the paper several times over. Those who have worked with young children will be familiar with those paintings that are so covered in paint that they have become a soggy hole! On occasions Jeanette placed another piece of paper over the top of her painting, often remarking, 'I've covered it up.' She once covered her painting with paper and pulled it apart to reveal a print of her original on the top paper. She said, 'I've made two, one for you and one for Mrs P. I'll put them together again,' showing her understanding and application of one-to-one correspondence and her attitude of giving her paintings to others as presents. Jeanette sometimes made her wet paintings into little presents, folding them into tiny 'parcels' which she took pleasure in presenting to interested adults. This will be familiar to many who know young chil-

dren. It is another 'excuse' to *enclose* and a childlike way of offering something special to others.

Jeanette dipped toy cars in paint, then moved them along the paper
making first an arc, then a straight line which almost connected the two
ends of the arc. She placed three cars inside the enclosure she had created
and said, 'Three cars in the car park' (Figure 4.4). The mathematical work
which Jeanette spontaneously undertook included organising space, using
numbers, thinking about size, shape, proportion and early tessellation. Action, graphic and speech representations were combined in this example.

As the examples of Jeanette's learning and development show, she
seemed to keep up a 'running commentary' of her work, often using language linked to the ideas of containing and enveloping. In further work,
Jeanette made some marks and covered them with another piece of card,
then secured them well with a large amount of sticky tape. When she was
apparently satisfied that sufficient tape had been used, she held up the card
and said, 'There, all covered up,' her smile indicating pleasure and satisfac-
tion in a job well done. She had learned about the materials she had used to
fasten her card. She had persevered for some time to develop a technique

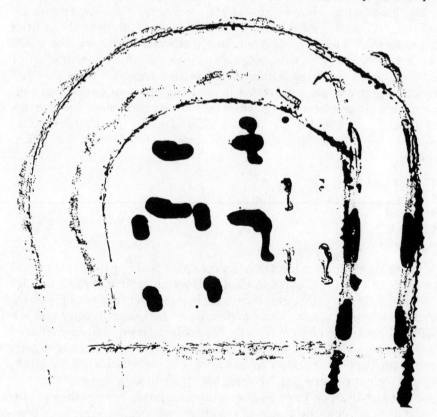

Figure 4.4 'Three cars in the car park'

that enabled her eventually, and with skill, to cut the tape without ending up with a sticky ball of useless tape and the belief that the material had a mind and will of its own!

Jeanette's interest in covering things extended to three-dimensional works. She wrapped cardboard tubes in paper and said they were 'crackers for a party'. The *form* of thought was enclosure, the *content* (in this instance) was party crackers. Jeanette filled paper bags with a variety of things: string, pieces of Lego, small pieces of shiny paper, clothes pegs. She gave one to each adult working in the nursery telling them, 'It's for you.' Jeanette was making and giving presents, but the learning underpinning this interaction of giving leads to ideas of degrees of fullness and emptiness, and to one-to-one correspondence. Jeanette was sure to fill one bag for each adult. Later she filled a plastic container with a similar collection of small objects and stuck on the lid. 'I helped Ben to make this present for his mum. I showed him how,' she said. (In fact, Ben had been allowed to watch Jeanette as she worked on the 'present' with industry. He was not permitted to do anything else to it!)

Further presents were made for a pretend party in the home corner. Books and small toys were collected from around the nursery and wrapped in sheets of paper. The will to and act of making and giving presents were as important a part of this little girl's affective development as was her learning related to areas of mathematical experience. On several occasions Jeanette seemed to derive pleasure in making something for – and giving it to – others.

Nursery teachers know that foundations of mathematical ideas of surface area, size and capacity can be laid in the process of early play with natural materials including water, sand and clay. These are essential materials in early education and used on a regular basis as part of a balanced range of curriculum opportunities. Provision of such natural materials, with a range of complementary equipment, gives children an open-ended resource with which to explore, discover, invent and create.

Water
Jeanette filled a jug with sponges and water, and this led to experiences of functional dependency (Athey, 1990, p. 70). Jeanette tried to make some plastic bottles stand up. They were empty and unstable, so fell over. She puzzled for a while and after repeated attempts to make them stand up said, 'Oh! I know why they won't stand up, 'cos they've no water in them, water makes them stand up.' She reasoned that the bottles standing upright were functionally dependent upon being filled with water.

Jeanette had created her own 'logical structure' and was able to reason and articulate her thinking (Piaget, 1972). Piaget considered the experience of objects to be a basic factor in the development of cognitive structures. He suggested that physical experience consists of acting upon, and drawing knowledge from, the results of these actions: knowledge being drawn not from the *objects* but from the *actions* that affected the objects (Stendler-Lavatelli and Stendler, 1972).

Sand

Jeanette filled a small bowl with pebbles and wet sand. She told her teacher, 'It's your dinner.' She continued to bury the 'dinner' in the sand: 'It has to go in the oven to cook, then you can get it out and eat it.' This happened a few days after the nursery had held a barbecue party in the garden attended by parents and other guests when potatoes wrapped in foil were placed in the barbecue fire to cook. Jeanette was perhaps drawing on this experience when she buried the sand 'dinner'. Real-life experiences of different ways of cooking and different kinds of food are a good source of curriculum content to nourish children's schemas.

Clay

Jeanette filled two containers with clay and declared, 'Shampoo and talc. It's a shop.' She later wrapped pieces of clay in some squares of brown paper and put them in a small box and closed the lid. 'I'm cooking the tea,' she said, 'it's a surprise tea tonight!' The underpinning *form of thought* (containing and enveloping) which was repeatedly apparent in Jeanette's learning and thinking was represented in different ways as she played with the clay.

Reflection on one level on the *content* of Jeanette's play and actions over time reveals a child who apparently flitted from one experience to another: house play, drawing, water, sand, clay, making crackers for an imaginary party, giving presents, playing at cooking. However, a focus on the underlying *form* of thinking present in these actions suggests that, far from flitting, she was systematically *fitting* together relevant experiences which matched her schematic interest. She selected from materials, activities and opportunities available to her a set of experiences which she bound together by an almost invisible thread of thinking. Athey discussed the notion of flitting and fitting:

> focusing on content at the expense of form can lead to the conclusion that young children flit from one theme to another and that they are unsystematic or even idiosyncratic . . . One of the uncharted areas of early cognitive functioning is children's own search for commonalities. While it is true that children often name a drawing as one thing and then change it to another, it is also true that, more often than not, there is a common form underlying differences in content.
>
> (Athey, 1990, p. 83)

Jeanette put herself inside spaces, covered spaces and places and filled spaces. At a basic *motor* level the containing and enveloping schemas were the structure within which she was learning about mathematical ideas of size, position, capacity, shape, quantity and space. These early motor experiences formed a basis for further development of these ideas when she met (or created for herself) similar and challenging situations. Much of Jeanette's work was self-motivated and appeared to involve significant learning steps.

Curriculum processes (whatever the current official requirements) must enable children to interact in this way with teachers and other professional early childhood educators, facilitating children's developmental knowledge and supporting their actions and discoveries. Teachers (and those who work in other state-funded forms of pre-school education) must adhere to official curriculum requirements which can form a basis for inspection, funding, assessment and accountability. But such requirements often represent a minimal form of provision for early learning and are no substitute for a high level of professional knowledge about elements of curriculum, child development and effective ways of challenging children's thinking.

Jeanette's explorations seemed to be systematic, fitting together as a cohesive, well-planned and relevant whole. This affirms the need to reconsider the notion that 4-year-olds have short concentration spans and only a limited ability to make choices for themselves. Jeanette was able to select from a wide range of experiences, to extend her thinking and to work in depth with adults who challenged, extended and supported her learning. Her graphic representations, actions, language and thought combined in common purpose. Jeanette's opportunities to explore her interests in the nursery depended upon the structure and curriculum of the nursery and the roles and skills of her teacher and other nursery staff.

Stuart: Dynamic circular schema

Stuart began nursery when he was just 3 years old. He lived in a mid-terraced council house 10 minutes' walk from the nursery, with his mother, grandmother and 2-month-old baby sister.

Stuart's interest in circular objects and movements fell into four categories identified by Athey (1990, p. 69): graphic representation (using marks or models); action representations (movement); speech representations; and functional dependency relationships. 'In early education *functional dependency relationships* are manifest when children observe the effects of action on objects or material. For example . . . melting wax is *functionally dependent* on heat' (*ibid.*, p. 70). It is sometimes helpful (though perhaps less technically precise) to understand this idea by thinking about simple cause-and-effect relationships. This would mean that the above example could be expressed as heat (the cause) makes wax melt (the effect). In the interests of accuracy and of consistency the words *functional dependency* will be used throughout.

Working at different levels on a dynamic circular schema, Stuart often used two kinds of representation together. Here, observations of Stuart will be discussed in terms of their representations (speech and graphic; action and speech; functional dependency relationships). These three categories of representations will be discussed in pairs because Stuart, like many 3-year-olds, often did more than one thing at once (therefore it is not surprising that different forms of representation occurred simultaneously). Stuart rarely played silently, either when he was alone or with others; he appeared to give a running commentary on his thinking and his actions. Because he was obligingly descriptive about what he was doing, this was a great help in interpreting his actions!

Speech and graphic representations of a circular schema

Stuart had little experience of using pens and paper before he began nursery. The marks he made in the early months following his third birthday were among his first. Some of Stuart's (3:2) early markmaking showed a predominance of circular motion. Many drawings looked similar to the examples in Figure 4.5 which he called *tractor wheels*. Three similar representations were named *Father Christmas, wheels-car* and *snake*. Such examples begin to illustrate early and uncomplicated representations, both through speech and graphic means, of a dynamic circular schema.

Sceptics will suggest that children make circular marks because the paper might suggest that shape, but a range of different sizes and shapes of paper were available, and when Stuart decided to paint, he made circular marks

Figure 4.5 'Tractor wheels'

on all the sheets he used, calling each one *snake*. Some children will follow the boundary suggested by the paper (another schema), but children are likely to pursue their schematic concerns and will be influenced by the shape of paper provided only if it matches their concerns and interests.

Stuart (3:3) chose some round shapes from a range of printing tools of different shapes and patterns. He used them to make several round marks and then, with a paintbrush, made large sweeping curves that encompassed the page. He said simply, 'Going round.' Later circular markmaking was labelled *mummy, daddy, Davey, Stuart, bike*.

Stuart was at the stage of using language to label things, so isolated words were more typical of his stage of language development than phrases or sentences. Interestingly, he used appropriate vocabulary to represent his schema through speech. The words *going round* were perhaps spoken by an adult working with Stuart to describe his actions as he painted. Stuart perhaps chose to repeat them later. If adults use appropriate descriptive language when working with children, language of *form* as well as appropriate *content* descriptions, children have the opportunity to obtain meaning from this kind of verbal 'match'.

Action and speech representations of a circular schema
When Stuart turned the handle of a hand-operated sewing machine (without a needle fitted!), action and speech representations were combined. He said, 'Going round.' He wound up a clockwork clock (a rare artefact in this digital microchip world), saying, 'Round and round.' He put cars on a sloping ramp of a toy garage and said, 'Look, round here, look wheels going round.' He used a cylindrical rotating puzzle and said, 'It goes round, look!'

Stuart seemed interested in the power of his own actions. He was absorbed with discovering what he could make happen, how he could make things behave. There was an extending role here for the adults who worked with Stuart, one which required inventiveness and quick thinking as well as sound knowledge of curriculum. When Stuart was using the hand-operated sewing machine, the teacher spoke about it with him:

Stuart: It goes round and round.
Teacher: Yes, it turns, it rotates.
Stuart: Then I stop it, I let it go.

It is apparent here that Stuart knew that he had some control over the machine. He had worked out for himself how it operated and what he needed to do to make the parts move. The dominant interest in this example was the *functional dependency relationship*. The movement of the wheel handle and the vertical action of the other part of the machine were functionally dependent upon Stuart operating the machine by turning the handle.

Adults can play a crucial role in extending and developing children's learning through identifying, understanding, supporting and extending their patterns of thinking. When Stuart (3:3) spent ten minutes spinning a rotating model with a figure of a person on one end and a weighted sphere on the other for balance, the teacher's interaction with him was finely tuned:

Stuart: Look, Look! Spinning, going round.
Teacher: It's rotating *(making a circular gesture with her hand)*.
Stuart: 'Tating, round and round, look, look! Spinning, 'tating, spinning.

Stuart was very excited by this, making circular hand gestures similar to those of the teacher. The teacher demonstrated that she valued Stuart's interest by matching her response to his comments and, in so doing, extending his vocabulary with different words to describe the movement of the model, and adding a hand gesture (another action representation) to accompany the word. Tait and Roberts (1974) discuss the technique of 'reflecting back'. In this case that technique was extended to introduce a new word as well as validate the words of the child, maintaining the child's meaning whilst extending the vocabulary. On other occasions Stuart's actions were used by the teacher in 'reflecting back' and providing a speech representation of his actions as a kind of accompanying dialogue. Going up the ramp outside, Stuart stopped and turned a full circle, he looked at the teacher who said: 'You went up and you turned right around.' Stuart replied, 'Right around.'

A key to the development of ideas and understanding can be a child's schema. When a Land Rover was driven into the nursery garden, Stuart spotted it and immediately sought a closer look. He found that he was not as tall as the large wheels on the vehicle (and so was on the appropriate level to examine them in detail). He commented with excitement, 'Look, big wheels, look!' Through an interest in things that rotated (and serendipity), his observational skills were heightened.

Functional dependency relationships

Stuart was talking with the teacher about round objects. The teacher was drawing his attention to different things in the environment, circular and otherwise:

Teacher: This fence has pieces of wood going up and down, this truck has wheels which go round and round.
Stuart: Like that *(making a circular gesture with his hand)*.
Teacher: Yes! Like that.
Stuart: Round and round and round.
Teacher: They rotate as they move along the ground.
Stuart: Rotate, go along, I like them.

Adults can introduce further extensions to schemas through such conversation. Stuart was clearly interested in *going round*. The teacher introduced the notion that going round was connected with going along. This could lead to future work with older children regarding circumference and land-measuring techniques. Curriculum issues will be discussed in Part III.

Functional dependency relationships can be reinforced in different ways; for example, many simple songs can help to support such understanding. While Stuart turned the handle of the sewing machine the teacher sang (to the tune of 'Here We Go Round the Mulberry Bu ' :

Sewing machine goes round and round,
Round and round, round and round,
Sewing machine goes round and round,
While Stuart turns the handle.

Stuart was able to identify functional dependency relationships by observing happenings in the nursery environment. He watched a joiner drilling a hole in a door in the nursery. Later he made a 'drill' using construction materials and 'worked' at the door. He explained, 'Goes round and round and round, goes zzz and makes that hole, look!'

Stuart made a drawing which represented this experience graphically, using vertical lines then a circular mark. He said: 'That's a man up on chair, doing it in.' As he said *doing it in*, he gestured as if holding the drill and drilling the hole. Stuart showed interest in a tool similar to that used by the joiner. The brace and bit was introduced to the woodwork tools to extend children's experiences of rotation and the consequent hole-making. After watching the real-life experience, Stuart spent some considerable time representing and repeating it using the woodwork equipment.

Nurseries, wherever possible, must provide a range of equipment which children can operate with developing confidence, skill, competence and imagination. Working with household equipment and tools that perform a real function can provide multiple opportunities to extend thinking and understanding.

What can we learn from Gary, Jeanette and Stuart?

The brief case studies of Gary, Jeanette and Stuart show how these children with different needs and at different stages of physical, cognitive and affective development were thinking and learning.

Glimpses into the experiences of these children show how concrete and realistic experiences (planned and serendipidous) can nourish the exploration of ideas – both fantastic and factual. The important role of real experience for Gary (the punctured tyre and the spider's web) is clear. The co-operative and tenacious venture of building the snow house illustrates how interests can be extended and developed in the outdoor environment, using spontaneous happenings and knowledge of children's interests to construct curriculum which is relevant and dynamic. Stuart's exchanges with his teacher reinforce the importance of nourishing children's language with relevant – finely tuned – adult talk.

Gary, Jeanette and Stuart worked at times independently and on other occasions in harmony with skilled and supportive adults. The potential for learning which 'fits' children's interests is clear.

This chapter has highlighted the learning processes which can occur from an open-ended and vibrant curriculum where children work in a carefully planned, finely tuned and 'well-stocked' environment and where appropriately trained, skilled and interested adults understand and use theories of how children learn. Later chapters will develop these issues.

Part III
Schemas and the development of knowledge and understanding

The next three chapters will examine and discuss children's early explorations of ideas which form the roots of mathematical and scientific development, children's patterns of literacy learning and the use of stories in extending children's knowledge and thought.

These topics have been chosen not because official documentation on curriculum and assessment gives them prominence (DfEE, 1996; QCA, 1997) but because there is much to understand about children's mathematical and scientific thinking – as *informed* by *children*, and because current attention to the literacy curriculum is in danger of neglecting *children's* attention to the written word in favour of – perhaps premature – prescribed teaching of, for example, letter formation. Stories too, are endangered in classrooms as they become misused as teaching aids good only for identification of particular phonic blends or elements of punctuation or grammar.

Throughout these three chapters run two themes. First, 'match' between children's *forms* of thought and curriculum *content* which enriches their learning. Second, the importance of reflection and evaluation of children's learning in 'matched' learning encounters.

5
CHILDREN'S DEVELOPING UNDERSTANDING OF MATHEMATICAL AND SCIENTIFIC IDEAS

Acceptance of the view that young children can and do learn as they pursue particular patterns of behaviour and interest requires a further step. That is, consideration of how such patterns (or schemas) might form part of the foundations of children's growing knowledge and understanding. This chapter presents the findings of research carried out in a nursery class in the mid-1980s. It suggests how children's pursuits of particular schemas can lead to the exploration of certain ideas and understandings. Observations of 40 children aged between 3 and 5 years were made during one academic year. Reflection upon the observations led to the identification of clusters of ideas being explored by the children. There were many examples of children pursuing interests with mathematical and scientific roots.

When the observations of children's actions were closely studied, it was evident that a rich variety of ideas was being investigated by the children. These included: capacity, tessellation, spatial order, size, shape, height, angles, perimeter, circumference, numbers, sorting, time, matching, quantity, position, estimation, transformation, addition, length, equivalence, distance, symmetry, properties of natural materials, cause, effect and functional relationships, centrifugal force, rotation, colour, magnetism, gravity, trajectory, natural science, change and speed.

Three major schemas emerged in the analysis of these observations: dynamic vertical, dynamic circular and enveloping/containing. From detailed interrogation of the observations came two generalisations:

- In each schema there emerged an idea that appeared to dominate.
- Some ideas were identified as arising from children's pursuit of all three schemas.

Three main questions were generated in an attempt to explain the observations. This chapter considers those questions in the light of the observations.

Do some ideas dominate in the pursuit of particular schemas?
From the observations of the children, three schemas revealed distinctive and, in a sense, obvious sets of ideas:

• The dynamic vertical schema was evident where some children were involved in activities and ideas concerned with height.
• Dynamic circular schema was evident where some children were exploring aspects of rotation and roundness.
• Containing/enveloping schemas were evident where instances of capacity were observed.

These three simple ideas are discussed next with examples of children's activity by way of illustration.

Dynamic vertical schema and ideas related to height

Emmie gained some experience of changes in height through repeated use of slide and steps. She said, 'I went up there and up there.' Her language included the idea of an increase in height and matched her actions.

Linda connected a number of bricks, one on top of the other. She said, 'It's a sword, I need a bit more to make it better.' Linda knew that she could increase the height of her construction by connecting more bricks and thereby, to her mind, improve it.

Lucy indicated that a ladder was a useful aid for increasing height when she said, 'That ladder is to go up.' Russell wanted to see out of the window so he put one brick on top of another and stood on them saying, 'I can see now I'm up here.' He had used his awareness and skills to make a step construction that would increase his height. This example reinforces the importance of motor actions and the relevance of *doing* as opposed to being told or explained to. Piaget (1953) emphasised that practical experiences were needed in order that understanding could occur and be demonstrated in a linguistic form.

William pretended to go up some stairs, lifting his feet as if mounting an imaginary staircase. He said, 'Up the stairs, up the stairs', then he turned and pretended to go down the stairs saying, 'Down the stairs, down the stairs.' It was as if language was a necessary part of the imagining. Later in the same month, William tried to climb onto the top of some 2-foot cubes which were piled up on a trestle platform. It was too high for him to manage and he could not reach the top. He fetched a stool and then a large brick which he used successfully to climb onto the top of the pile. He said, 'There are two steps, one big one and one little one.'

William had constructed a map of understanding about size and increase in height that meant that he could eventually solve his problem. The development of thinking and problem-solving strategies should be fostered by open-ended experiences of infinite variety and frequency which involve children in creating and seeking solutions to their problems. The responsibility of the professional educator is to provide the opportunity and work with the children who will, with support, challenge and encouragement, solve their problems.

HMI identified four main areas in which children need to develop scientific skills:

1. making and recording observations;
2. identifying patterns;
3. developing hypotheses;
4. investigating and experimenting.

They stated:

> For the youngest children many scientific interests begin with exploratory play. In nursery and infant classes children frequently demonstrate an ability to explain their observations and test their ideas as they take part in early scientific activities . . . Work with sand and water . . . and activities involving constructional materials such as wooden bricks and toys with moving parts invariably involve children in investigations that lead them to explain scientific phenomena and sequences of events as far as their understanding allows.
>
> (DES, 1989b, para. 57)

Unfortunately, though mathematical understanding is given a high degree of prominence in more recent government documents, there is less emphasis on play and more on 'teaching' and the acquisition of specifically identified 'skills':

> The Desirable Outcomes are goals for learning for children by the time they enter compulsory education. They emphasise early literacy, numeracy and the development of personal and social skills and contribute to children's knowledge, understanding and skills in other areas. Presented as six areas of learning, they provide a foundation for later achievement.
>
> (DfEE, 1996, p. 1)

The dynamic circular schema and the development of ideas about rotation

Frances showed some considerable interest in rotation. She seemed intrigued by objects that rolled, and by the rotation of an old record-player turntable. She chose two model elephants, one larger than the other, and placed them on the turntable. Frances set the turntable in motion and said, 'The baby elephant is chasing the daddy,' then she laughed and said, 'The daddy is chasing the baby too!' As Frances described her observation, she conceptualised the notion of rotation and circular action. Chapman and Foot (1976) considered that humour in infancy is characterised mainly by the way children are amused by things they understand. Humour, they say, is related to cognition. Frances had some sense of the 'circleness' of a circle, never really ending or beginning, and her understanding led to her amusement.

Frances's teacher, believing that her schematic interest was clear, developed activities in ways which supported her schematic interests and extended her learning. On one occasion this involved Frances and two other children helping to make pumpkin soup. The equipment used for this included a can opener, pepper and salt mills, and an electric liquidiser.

Frances found the liquidiser fascinating, observing that, 'It's spinning faster and faster and making the big bits little.' Using language related to rotation, she described the process she saw and included a comment on two important basic concepts, *change* and *size*. She investigated the salt and pepper mills, and seemed delighted to discover how they worked. The mills provided more experience of rotation and of cause, effect and functional relationships. Frances carefully turned the handle of the can opener, noting that: 'If you turn this handle, the tin turns too; and if you keep turning, the lid comes right off.'

Through her interest in rotation Frances was grappling with the principles of cause and effect, learning about what made things happen; what is more, she was able to use language to articulate what she saw and thought. She included in her talk the vocabulary of rotation, matching her words to the things she saw and making some precise comments. As well as using the kitchen tools competently and with understanding of how they worked, Frances remembered to stir the soup frequently, watching the circular pattern the stirring made. The task of making soup for a winter party was a real job and suitable equipment was selected to extend the related learning opportunities involved.

Frances (with the support of the teacher) appeared absorbed for the whole of the hour it took to make the soup. The two other children quickly lost interest and left the activity; other children came and went, but Frances remained involved and actively interested until the soup was ready to eat. This example highlights the need for available and informed adults to give intensive one-to-one attention to children's learning opportunities, through their finely tuned interactions with individual children.

Why did Frances stick at making the soup for so long? Might the prolonged concentration be linked to a match between a child's schema and the task at hand? Suggestions that young children can only concentrate for short periods and have a low level of persistence have been disputed for some time. Young children, time and time again, prove themselves capable of serious persistence when the work in which they are involved matches their interests.

Other children in the same nursery were interested in rotation:

- David spent fifteen minutes turning the blades on a small toy helicopter.
- Gary turned the handle on an unconnected tap and later found a rotary spinning toy and asked how it worked. He spent time spinning it and exploring the action it made.
- Guy demonstrated his interest in rotation when he painted pictures of a washing machine. He said, 'They're clothes going round and round and

getting clean.' His experience of technology in the real world enabled him to add to and represent his understanding of rotation in a creative medium and through appropriate language.

John was interested in how things worked. He was sorting through a collection of metal objects and found a screw. He took it to the teacher and said, 'Here's a screw.' The teacher asked what it was for and John replied, 'A screw driver,' making a circular gesture with his hand as if using a screwdriver. John was combining his knowledge of what goes with what (one-to-one correspondence) and function (the screwdriver makes the screw go into the wood), linked perhaps through his interest in finding things that rotated. John found a brass tap, he turned the nut at one end until it came off; then he turned the handle. Through these actions John gained more feedback and information about rotation and its effect on objects.

Guy found three wooden circles and said, 'Oh! More rounds!' In so doing, he showed that he could identify the shape and classify them as part of a set. He used the language of addition, 'more', to indicate his discovery. Guy later found a small wheel and said, 'There's another wheel here, I've got these, that's one and that's another one.' He was adding to his collection of circular items and reinforcing his own ideas of addition and using a range of mathematical terms.

At this point it is perhaps worth mentioning the importance of creating opportunities for seemingly incidental mathematical discovery. Discussing the development of mathematical concepts in the nursery, Matthews (1984) considered the use of mathematical terms such as 'more', 'not enough', 'bigger' and 'fit' in spontaneous experiences, to be the best method of facilitating mathematical development. As has been stated many times, and discovered by most human beings, 'finding out' can, at every age, often lead to more meaningful learning than 'being told'. However, it is still necessary to repeat the mantra because it is not as readily applied to official constructions of curriculum as it might be.

Containing and enveloping schemas and the development of knowledge of capacity

Writing about the beginnings of measurement, Dowling states:

> For young children to learn how to measure accurately they need a range of experiences in making judgements about amounts . . . This happens through children handling materials and conversing with one another, suggesting who has more or less milk or who has collected bigger stones. Children need to judge how much paper or material they require to cover a surface, and the teacher may join in at this stage to ask if the amount is too large or too little.
>
> (Dowling, 1988, p. 46)

Many of the observations that inform this book feature children exploring ideas related to capacity and volume through the use of a variety of materials either to contain objects or to envelop spaces (by covering or surrounding). Children used natural materials, construction tools, the home corner and imaginative play props to develop ideas of containing and capacity.

Adam used sand and water to fill or cover objects and containers. Frances filled bottles with water and poured from small bottles into larger ones, thus experiencing capacity in relation to the size of an object. Kelly made her own paper container and used what was at hand in the nursery to create her experience of volume when she wrapped sand, string and dry spaghetti in a paper parcel.

In the home corner, Lulu sorted plates, saucers and cups into a drawer. Not only did she fit the objects into a space (thus gaining experience of capacity), she also sorted and classified those objects. Later she placed some small plastic shapes in a container, in that simple action adding to her experience of containers and containing; and so expanding her concept of volume.

Guy found an open-mouthed toy monster that he began to fill with small pieces of Lego, using things he found readily available to continue his interest. Athey (1990) notes that children will use whatever they can find to extend their schemas. This being the case, questions inevitably arise about appropriate provision and curriculum content. Chapter 8 considers those issues.

What other ideas do children explore whilst pursuing particular schemas?

The observations of the 40 children suggested that, as well as exploring the ideas already discussed, other ideas were encountered as children pursued particular schemas.

Particular experiences arising from children's pursuit of dynamic vertical and straight-line schemas

As some children explored ideas of height, they encountered challenges which led to increased awareness of length, equivalence, distance and symmetry. Such experiences were only identified in observations where children showed a strong interest in vertical and straight-line schemas.

Adam fitted construction pieces end to end, and placed them between the tables on the nursery floor to make a long line. In so doing, Adam was working with concepts of length and space. He saw that he could add more pieces to increase length, and looking at his work he saw the length of what he had made in comparison with the floor.

David and Saul used the climbing frame, walking up the slide, turning and running down, then later using the steps to ascend and descending by way of the slide. These children were experiencing asymmetry of movement as well as developing their growing bodies.

Gerry walked to the top of the yard and rode down the slope on a truck. This basic motor-level experience provided potential for understanding and experience of the equivalence of distance and comparison of speed, since walking up took him longer than riding down, even though the distance travelled each time was the same. A similar experience occurred when Gerry crawled from one end of a platform to the other and then ran back along the outside. This too allowed him to experience equivalence of distance and difference in speed. Young children have the opportunity to build some of their own foundations for mathematical and scientific understanding through such experience. The validity and relevance of these kinds of experiences need to be emphasised and recognised in terms of their potential for learning, but outdoor play and physical experiences of running, climbing, crawling and bike riding are not identified as sources of mathematical and scientific learning as often as they might be. The detail of children's activities and their thinking can be lost if adults do not observe the children they work with and make sense of those observations in terms of how young children learn. As Dowling (1988, p.45) puts it, 'The nursery can thus provide a seedbed for mathematical thinking. A range of potentially helpful activity can be explored, but as with other aspects of development the cue must come mainly from the child. These cues need to be observed, then taken up and developed by the teacher.'

Particular experiences arising from the dynamic circular schema

As well as exploring ideas of rotation, activities leading to experiences in the areas of transformation and change were also identified in observations indicating a dynamic circular schema.

Colin chose cups, dishes, a jug and plates in the home corner and systematically turned each one upside down on the table, thus transforming the objects to give a different configuration. Colin saw what he had done, the change he had created by turning each object through 180°.

The example of Frances making the pumpkin soup (earlier in this chapter) provides another example of children's use of mathematical and scientific language. Describing the effect of the liquidiser on the food inside it she said, 'It's spinning faster and faster and making the big bits little.' Her understanding of the term *faster* is clear as is her appreciation of the effect of increasing speed on the changing size of the food.

Particular experiences arising from containing/enveloping schemas

Ideas of capacity arising from children's exploration of containing and enveloping schemas have already been discussed. A great variety of experiences can support the further development of ideas such as corners and angles, position, estimation, space and place which are also evident through children's exploration of containing/enveloping schemas.

Frances used the term *corner* when she played with the doll's house, placing different pieces of furniture into all the corner spaces of the rooms. What she *did* indicated that she understood what she *said*. Lucy sat in a corner and then placed a doll's bath in a corner of the doll's house. As these children interacted with and manipulated their environments, they were both experiencing 'cornerness', and through such physical experiences would be in a position later to understand more abstract ideas of corners and angles.

Seb buried a toy in the sand. 'It's on this side,' he said, giving another child a clue about where to find it. Seb knew that there was *another* side and drew on his understanding of position and perspective in order to create his clue.

Observations of these children suggest that the beginnings of ideas about perimeter and area are closely linked with children's graphic representation. Lulu and Lucy both enclosed spaces with paint, painting around the edges of their paper. Linda used ribbon similarly to edge a piece of card. Mathematics, it seems, is never far away from young children's actions. Fontana (1984) considered mathematics to be present in the selection of materials for collage, in the home corner, in stories and in music. Mathematical ideas are not only present in children's choices and selections of materials but also in the ways they use the materials available to them. How children use materials can impact on the learning potential of what is done.

When Frances was trying to build a house of large bricks, she demonstrated her ability to estimate. Part-way through the construction, she looked at her building and at the remaining bricks. 'There's no more bricks to build a house, there's not enough.' She had not counted the bricks but could see that the remaining materials were insufficient to complete the task. Early play is vital to future mathematical development (Hodgkin, 1985) and the importance of blockplay in the development of children's mathematical and scientific ideas has been highlighted by the Froebel Blockplay Project (Gura, 1992). But *breadth* and *depth* of experience are fundamental. Narrow mathematical objectives such as those published in 1996 (DfEE) could have the effect of restricting mathematical and scientific 'thinking' in order to boost a discrete set of skills.

Guy used a puzzle that entailed fitting cylinders into holes. He counted 'One, two, three, four' then he placed a cylinder in each hole. He employed his knowledge of numbers, the language of number and one-to-one correspondence to complete the self-chosen task. Susan was wrapping a parcel. Her understanding of size, classification and numbers was apparent when she said, 'I'll put a big one and two small ones in this parcel.'

Saul's matching skills were apparent when he looked at some construction plans and asked another child to 'make a house like that one'. The language 'like that' is indicative of children's developing mathematical appreciation of comparison, similarity and difference. HMI asserted the importance of teaching children in ways that encourage them to talk mathematically:

> Their [children's] ability to use mathematical language discriminatingly and accurately is increased through well-planned practical activities and play experiences designed to help them understand aspects of number, weight, size, capacity, time and measurement.
>
> (DES, 1989a, para. 39)

In 1996 emphasis on mathematics before school was described thus:

> These outcomes cover important aspects of mathematical understanding and provide the foundation for numeracy. They focus on achievement through practical activities and on using and understanding language in the development of simple mathematical ideas.
>
> Children use mathematical language, such as circle, in front of, bigger than and more, to describe shape, position, size and quantity. They recognise and recreate patterns. They are familiar with number rhymes, songs, stories, counting games and activities. They compare, sort, match, order, sequence and count using everyday objects. They recognise and use numbers to 10 and are familiar with larger numbers from their everyday lives. They begin to use their developing mathematical understanding to solve practical problems. Through practical activities children understand and record numbers, begin to show awareness of number operations, such as addition and subtraction, and begin to use the language involved.
>
> (DfEE, 1996, p. 3)

Lucy pursued her containing/enveloping schemas through imaginative play and construction. She built a house with large wooden bricks. There was no opening. She reflected and said, 'There's no doorway,' but this did not seem to concern her; she put a variety of objects into the house and seemed to enjoy being inside the house herself. She commented, 'Only one more can come in, there's not much space.' Lucy was using language related to containing and mathematics, and through her actions and words, demonstrated knowledge of number, quantity, size, position, space and estimation. Later, at Lucy's request the teacher provided boxes to improvise as a bath and a washing machine and Lucy put a doll in the 'bath' and dolls clothes into the 'washing machine'. Lucy then dressed the doll, using her finely developed manipulative skills for this different kind of enveloping. She decided that the clothes were still wet and needed to be put in 'the tumbler' to dry. She asked the teacher for sticky tape, 'because I want the clothes to stay in,' she explained, again using language related to containing.

Lucy enclosed a variety of objects in several different ways and for different purposes, using the teacher as a provider of resources to develop and extend her play.

On different occasions Lucy used a range of materials to build houses for make-believe and miniature people. For example, she attached a garage to her house and put a truck inside it. 'They're all inside that truck in the garage,' she said. Later she put the people inside the house: 'People are in the rooms, that's where they live, that ladder is to get up, when they're up they can get in there and go to bed.' Here she was combining ideas of going up with ideas of *going in*, using appropriate language to describe her thinking.

Are some similar ideas developed as children explore different schemas?

Observations of the 40 children in the study showed that some mathematical and scientific ideas arose from all three schemas: dynamic vertical, dynamic circular and containing/enveloping. These include: capacity; tessellation; spatial order; surface area; shape; sorting; cause, effect and functional relationships; and colour.

Children's ideas about and experiences of capacity have already been discussed. The discussion in this section will focus on aspects of children's thinking and understanding in three of the areas listed above: tessellation; cause, effect and functional relationships; and surface area. These have been chosen because they relate to aspects of learning not often discussed in relation to the development of children aged 3 and 4 years. The areas that will be given less attention in this discussion are sorting, size, colour and shape. These are ideas already fully established as fundamental in the early years curriculum (Fontana, 1984).

Tessellation and spatial order

Examples of children's exploration and understanding of tessellation and positioning indicate the capability of young children to focus on some complex mathematical ideas. Guy chose a wooden puzzle and fitted shaped bricks together to fill the outline. Some days later he fitted squares of wood together on a large sheet of paper. A week later he arranged four footballs together on a square and kicked one, which had the effect of moving all four. He exclaimed, 'They go all over!' It is possible that Guy was aware of the ways in which two-dimensional shapes fitted together and was experimenting with the tessellation of three-dimensional shapes. He watched a bricklayer who was working in the nursery garden, observing with interest the tessellation of bricks of the same shape and size as they were fitted together in different ways to form a pillar.

Leo piled six one-foot cubes on top of one another against the brick wall alongside. He later extended his earlier attempt, building the cubes three high and two deep. Lulu used paint to mark a grid pattern on a large sheet of paper, producing an example of tessellating squares. She later used various shapes to make a printed design where different shapes fitted together.

Guy, Leo and Lulu used available equipment to develop their own individual experiences. They manoeuvred and organised shapes and space.

Piaget and Inhelder (1956) noted that children's early concepts of space were topological, later giving way to Euclidean concepts. Ideas of space can be difficult for educators to understand and discuss, but some understanding is important if children's understanding of space is to be fully nurtured. Helpful definitions and examples of types of space are given by Dickson, Brown and Gibson (1993). They describe topological properties as 'global properties which are independent of size or shape' (p. 13) and Euclidean properties as 'those relating to size, distance and direction and hence leading to the measurement of lengths, angles, areas and so on' (p. 14).

Children explore space in flexible ways: manipulating shapes into spaces; arranging shapes into regular and irregular patterns; and creating patterns in space as they draw and paint. In the light of such varied manipulation of shape and space, the usefulness of jigsaws that require children to fit shapes together in a single set fashion, and colouring books that offer only the opportunity to fill in fixed spaces of colour, need to be questioned. How do such activities support and nourish the ideas of flexible space?

Surface area

Sally seemed to be interested in ideas and experiences involving vertical movement. She painted, moving the brush up and down on the page to create patches of colour until she had covered the whole page with red paint. Given materials and time, young children can create their own experiences – of covering space. Educators must recognise the value of such use of paint and of children's time for the learning opportunity it provides. Saul made a similar painting using circular actions and marks to fill his page, eventually producing a page covered with orange paint. The detail of the processes involved here would not be discernable from simply looking at the final product. Observation of children *as they work* are essential to effective learning.

Many examples of children's experiences of surface area came about when children covered themselves, or each other. Fiona put an adult into bed in the home corner and covered her up. Fiona incorporated mathematical ideas into her imaginative play. She realised that she needed to use two sheets to cover the teacher because one sheet was not long enough (even though one sheet was usually all that was needed to cover up other children).

Gwen found a piece of wrapping paper, and looked at a small farm building, seemingly intending to wrap it in the paper. 'Not big enough,' she said and looked for a bigger sheet of paper. Finding none, she then chose a smaller item to wrap! Gwen was able to estimate size and had an idea of the relationship between the size of a three-dimensional object and the two-dimensional size of paper required to wrap it. She concluded her activity by singing 'Happy birthday' thus incorporating make-believe and the meaning of events such as present-giving into her work.

Cause, effect and functional relationships

Children are interested in the outcomes of their own actions. Many of the children represented in this book were fascinated with how things worked and what *they* could make things do. The following examples illustrate how children can investigate and deduce the function of an object and then articulate what they do with appropriate language.

Gail was turning the handle of a vice on the woodwork bench. She said, 'Look, when I turn it [the handle] that comes out and I can get the wood in.' She had deduced the function of the vice through manipulation, experimentation and observation. Four weeks later, Gail took a container to the sink and filled it with water. The water continually poured out of the container and (after many unsuccessful attempts) Gail eventually discarded it. She remarked, 'It's got little holes in so the water will always go on the floor.' She clearly understood the effect of holes on the ability of the container to hold water, that this was not a 'one-off' occurrence, and any container with holes always fails to hold water.

Ann turned the handle on a toy garage and said, 'When I turn this, that bit over there moves and when the car is on it, it turns around.' She described quite clearly the cause (turning the handle) and the effect (movement of a small platform), and the function (turning a car around).

Lulu watched a tin cylinder roll off the table and said, 'This is silly, it fell down there because it's round.' Having understood the action of the rolling tin, she had the basis of her own hypothesis that round things roll.

As children talk, as they manipulate their words and create different meanings, they often display their understandings of cause, effect and functional relationships. It is difficult to know whether children understand cause-and-effect relationships if they do not articulate their thinking. It is a responsibility of teachers and other educators to include children in discussions that feature different terminology so that children can build on these modelled vocabularies and generate the words they need to talk about their own findings and ideas. The needs of bilingual children must be addressed in this context, with opportunities for all children to develop and discuss their ideas through their home language.

Carol put a water pump into the water and seemed fascinated by the up-and-down action she made. Her understanding of the relationship between her actions and the pumping of the water is not clear because she said nothing, but the teacher watched her, moved close beside her, and described what Carol was doing: 'You're moving the pump handle up and down and it fills with water and the water is coming out of the top.' The teacher's description was designed to help Carol understand what she did and saw and provide words for her to use herself should she choose to. Teachers can introduce the language of cause and effect in this way, saying things like 'it's doing that because' or 'that's why . . .'

Three questions about schemas and the development of children's mathematical and scientific ideas have been considered here. What is clear from the observations of the forty 3–5-year-old children represented in this study is that such children can acquire a wealth of knowledge and understanding that enables them to develop a command over a range of mathematical and scientific ideas:

> It is the basic themes that lie at the heart of Science and Mathematics and the basic themes that give form to life and literature are as simple as they are powerful. To be in command of these basic ideas, to use them effectively, requires a continual deepening of one's understanding of them that comes from learning to use them in progressively more complex forms. It is only when such basic ideas are put in formalised terms as equations or elaborated verbal concepts that they are out of reach of the young child, if he has not first understood them intuitively and had a chance to try them out on his own. The early teaching of Science, Mathematics, Social Studies and literature should be designed to teach these subjects with scrupulous intellectual honesty, but with an emphasis upon the intuitive grasp of ideas and upon the use of these basic ideas.
>
> (Bruner, 1977, p. 12)

The children's learning described in this chapter has its own 'intellectual honesty', derived as it is from an extensive range of activities rooted mostly in children's play. The range and depth of experiences provided in the nursery challenged children to think. For teachers and other staff responsible for the development of children's minds, the challenge was to provide for children according to their individual capabilities and interests.

This chapter has examined ways in which children can develop understanding of mathematical and scientific ideas through first-hand experiences and a furtherance of their schemas. It has illustrated how action, thinking and language are inextricably linked in the processes of generating and developing ideas and understanding. The learning discussed in this chapter is that of children who embarked on dynamic exploration and discovery. They were active participants in their learning process, facilitated according to their individual learning patterns. Extensive opportunities were provided by knowledgeable professionals who understood children and their ways of learning. Some issues raised in this chapter have implications for curriculum provision which will be discussed in Chapter 8.

6
PATTERNS OF LITERACY

Razia and four other children who began school the term before their fifth birthdays were playing in the 'office' that was set up just outside the reception class. The office was equipped with two typewriters, one manual, one electric, a computer set up with a word-processing package and a concept keyboard, several telephones, a working intercom between the classroom and the office, note pads, order books, pens, catalogues, envelopes, 'in' and 'out' trays, and other office paraphernalia. The children had been to the school office to see the equipment in use and they had also, in small groups, visited the large offices of a local business.

Picture Razia, aged 4 years and 8 months. She was sitting at the typewriter, typing a page of notes from her note pad. She was having some difficulty 'reading' from the writing on her pad. 'If this was on tape it would be much easier – I can't read her writing!' This was probably a reference to something a secretary told her when she went to the local office, about how difficult it sometimes was to read people's handwriting and how it was often easier if they dictated their letters onto tape using a dictaphone.

Another child told her that there was a telephone call for her and passed her the telephone. Razia tucked it between her chin and right shoulder and continued to type whilst she spoke to the caller! Then she took a pen in her left hand and scribbled a note on her pad. 'Yes, yes OK, I'll tell her. Thank you for calling.' Razia replaced the telephone and finished writing the message. In her play, this little girl reflected some of what she had learned about how some people work, how they communicate, the words they use, the postures they assume and that office life can be very busy.

Literacy learning in school can have a real purpose and context, and experience can often be the motivation for new learning. Literacy and play go hand in hand for many young children (Christie, 1991). Razia, a developing writer and reader, already knew how useful these abilities were and wanted to use what she knew about reading and writing in her play. Her playing had such purpose, grounded as it was in real-life experiences, but what would her teacher do to challenge and extend Razia's literacy even further?

Razia had spent most of the morning in the office play area and now the teacher wanted to spend some time writing with her and giving her some individual teaching time. Razia, however, was engrossed, her language was flowing, something the teacher wanted to encourage in this young bilingual child. The teacher drew on what she saw, and what she knew about children's development and learning and her own experience of effective pedagogy, to help her decide her next step. She needed to make certain that her *intervention* did not become *interference* in Razia's thinking and learning processes. She wanted to enhance existing learning, not to interrupt it. The teacher approached Razia with some 'typing'. 'Razia, could you type a letter for me please? I want to write to the office to say "Thank you" for letting us visit. If you type it, everyone could sign it and then it can be posted – we'll need an envelope too.' Razia glowed with pride at the prospect of the task. She had a sense of purpose. She set to work immediately and typed the letter, which had been drafted by the teacher, following through the task by getting children to sign their names at the bottom of the letter, in conventional style. She selected a brown envelope and typed 'OFIS' on the front. The teacher wrote a 'covering letter' to accompany Razia's, in case the office staff were not conversant in emergent typing!

Razia and her teacher were engaged in a dynamic teaching and learning process, grown out of real situations and leading to purposeful outcomes. Razia gained more experience of focusing on writing and identifying individual letters; she made a good attempt at reading the teacher's letter and had a clear understanding of what she was typing. She identified individual letters and some whole words and was able to find the letters she needed on the typewriter keyboard. Children can be motivated when creative. Flexible teachers provide them with real purposes, real tasks and real audiences, and are prepared to adapt their learning objectives for children when necessary. Razia's teacher moulded her teaching to the child's present interest, and in so doing successfully focused the child on aspects of writing. She did not accomplish this by requiring the *child* to adapt to the teacher's pre-planned agenda. 'Moulding' teaching into children's interests can make for effective moments of learning.

What did Razia learn by being asked to type the letter? She learned that she and her contributions to the task were valued by the teacher. She learned a little more about communicating with others, conventions of saying 'Thank you' to their hosts, and she learned that her letter was worth writing and worth sending. It had a place – a rightful place – in the world of words and letters. She sensed real purpose and real achievement. She used capital and lower case letters as appropriate. She checked her typed version against the teacher's draft. She wrote her name correctly. These are some of the essential building blocks of early literacy.

How is Razia's teacher supporting and extending her development? How does she decide on her role? The framework set out in Figure 6.1 is a useful way to define the role of the teacher in encouraging children's emergent writing.

Give children rich and varied models of literacy, in a variety of settings: shops, offices, homes, schools, printers, leisure centres. Let them see people using their literacy skills and tools to communicate with others. As Wray

```
MODEL

PROVIDE

OBSERVE

INTERACT

INTERVENE

EVALUATE
```

Figure 6.1 Framework for encouraging emergent literacy

suggests, children need to see literacy happening: 'A literate environment is a fairly meaningless concept without people who are using that environment, people who, through a variety of ways in which they use print, demonstrate when it is used, how it is used, where it is used and what it is' (Wray, Bloom and Hall, 1989, p. 66).

Children need dynamic opportunities to write in context. Readers and writers can flourish when a variety of models of literacy are presented to children and when the literacy environment is richly provided for. Teachers and other early childhood educators must first consider what children *know* about literacy and what kinds of *models* of literacy they are familiar with. They must *provide* opportunities for children to write and to read, and the equipment and materials they need to do this: quality books (as discussed in the next chapter), writing tools, examples of print and the written word in a variety of scripts and fonts.

Those who work with young children must employ their skills of *observation,* watching what children do and say, assessing what children know and deciding where they might need help. Observation helps educators to decide what to do next in terms of supporting, developing and extending children's development as writers and readers. As well as observing what children do and say in terms of literacy, *interaction* with children as they read and write is all-important. Observation and interaction can help to determine the nature of *intervention* on the part of the educator. To make certain that positive intervention does not become futile interference in a child's learning process, it must be preceded by sensitive observation and interaction with the child. All of this takes a high level of skill and knowledge about young children and how they react and act in different circumstances. This framework for the educator requires knowledge about literacy and a sense of progression in literacy acquisition, achieved through ongoing professional development, dialogue with others and a critical knowledge of research, policy and practice. The practical framework of *model, provide, observe, interact, intervene* is not complete without the educator's *evaluation.* There must be a time for reflection upon what happened, and an assessment, however brief, of the strategies used and the resulting outcomes. Questions need to be asked such as: What did Razia learn? Was the teacher's strategy a successful one? What will the teacher do next?

Much has been written about the development of children as writers. The National Writing Project (1989) provided clear and accessible accounts of children's early development of writing systems. There are also several studies which document in fine detail the early writing development of individual children (Payton, 1984; Bissex, 1980; Schickedanz, 1990). A booklet *Writing for All* (Oldham LEA, 1992) stresses that children with special educational needs are entitled to be taught to write in the same way as pupils in mainstream schooling, and suggests that there are three main elements to becoming a writer: composer (creating meaning); communicator (conveying meaning); and secretary (markmaking). It is when all three elements are supported and developed effectively through interactive teaching and learning processes that children emerge as competent and confident writers. The introduction of the National Literacy Strategy (DfEE, 1998) designed to improve literacy teaching and raise standards of literacy in primary schools, has – ironically – given rise to fears that children's early literacy development might suffer as a result of over-prescriptive lessons and decontextualised literacy activities. There are worries too that the place of play in early literacy teaching and learning is being eroded – history and the experiences of teachers and children will tell, but in assessing results it will be important to measure those elements of literacy that matter most.

Two questions can be asked about children's schemas and their writing development. These concern the *form* and *content* of writing.

- First, should the *form* and the *content* of writing be given separate and different value and attention?
- Second, are there links between the *form* and *content* of young children's writing and other underpinning threads of children's thought and action?

Form and content in young children's early writing

If the voices of children are to be valued, the content of their writing, the essence of its *meaning* and its *focus* must always be important. What children choose to say in their writing, why they write, for whom they write, are important elements in the making of a writer. The content of children's writing will be influenced by the experiences they have and what they find meaningful. Children's writing often reflects events which are important to them, real and imagined happenings, the plots from favourite or influential stories they have read or heard told to them.

In parallel with children's development as authors, and the creation of meaning through their writing, is development of what might be described as 'secretarial skills', which include the understanding children show in their early markmaking of what a writing system is about: signs, symbols, conventions. Early attempts to write words and letter-like symbols are useful evidence of learning about the *form* that writing takes and the structure of a writing system. Young, developing bilingual and multilingual children are often representing symbols and creating strategies to understand, and use several scripts which have different signs and different conventions (Hirst, 1998).

The *form* and *content* of children's writing are both important factors in the making of a writer. *Form* is about structure and presentation whilst *content* represents the essence and meaning of a writer's writing. Good teachers can help children to develop both aspects of writing in parallel. Well-formed, legible marks which have nothing to communicate are of little use. Writers only become writers when they have something to say. *Form* without meaning is wasteful of effort, whilst children who have plenty to say but cannot grasp the literacy strategies of *form* to help them say it will struggle. Neither form nor content should be sacrificed in the interests of the other, and both must be nurtured.

National strategy appears to have influenced an increasing emphasis on getting the *form* of writing correct at the expense of listening to the messages children have to convey through writing. There is emphasis on correctness of form in the National Curriculum where, by the age of 7, children should have considerable control over handwriting form. Though there is also a requirement that children should write in an interesting way, there is a danger that things which are more easily assessed, such as the correct position of capital letters and full stops, are given greater value than children's ability to convey their own clearly personal meanings in their compositions. This was well argued by Armstrong (1990, p. 15), who demonstrated the belief that meaning must be held central to children's writing. He observed: 'One of the most important tasks in interpreting children's work is to describe its patterns of intention: the interests, motifs, orientations, forms of meditation that govern a child's thought and seek expression in her practice.' As teachers work to implement the National Literacy Strategy (DfEE, 1998) in classrooms, it will remain imperative that children are encouraged to communicate their own personal and vital stories and messages in their writing. This is as essential to becoming a writer as attention to correctness of grammar and presentation – perhaps, in human terms more so. Attention must be paid to the content of each child's writing if their 'voice' and the meaning of their writing and thinking is to be valued.

Links between writing form and content and other areas of children's thought and action

Might it be possible to identify links between the form and content of young children's writing and other underpinning threads of children's thought and action? Sophie (7.5) was writing about a train ride. The content of her writing included several references to *connections*: a tunnel; gates at the station; stepping-stones across a river. There was an apparent link with her self-motivated interest in 'joined-up' writing and the connection of letters (and words). Her teacher explained that the class as a whole had not yet tackled joined-up writing, but that Sophie seemed intent on joining not only letters within words but also linking the words together! This interest in *connection* linked with her interests in art and dance, where she incorporated content related to joining and connecting.

Angie (4.2) drew a picture which appeared to the teacher to be a single block of colour. In her description of the picture she included several references to coverings. Angie illuminated the thinking her pictures represented as she labelled parts of her drawing:

That's the house.
That's the little girl covered in paint.
That's the rain dropping down.
This is snow. The snow will be covered up with rain.
That's rain dropping down on to it and covers over the snow.

Angie's description included several references to covering, suggesting a link between her thinking and her representations in drawing and speech.

Writing as representation

The idea of writing as a means of representation is another aspect of writing development which needs consideration.

Writing representing writing

As they begin to pay attention to the *act* of writing, young children seem to write 'for the sake of it'. They move their pen quickly across the page, as they have perhaps seen their mother do when she writes a quick letter, seated at the kitchen table. They might produce a series of linear squiggles which represents the *look* of writing and, in the act of doing this, they get the *feel* of being a writer. Adults who watch young children at this stage of their writing development will notice that children assume the posture and demeanour of a writer; they 'write' with intensity, their faces show concentration and they 'write' with a certainty of focus and purpose. A child who writes in this way might produce something similar to that in Figure 6.2. Adam (3:2), who did this, looked up at his mother and said, 'I'm writing.' He was, it seemed, representing the *act* of writing, the process, the 'feel' – rather than the 'product' of writing.

The child who knows a little more about marks which make up writing may write something similar to the example in Figure 6.3. When Joanne (4:4) wrote this she said, 'This is writing.' She used what she knew about writing and writing conventions to produce a page of symbols which looked like writing. There was no message as such, it simply *was* writing.

Some children know the power of the written word and can produce writing which has influential content before they have developed sufficient

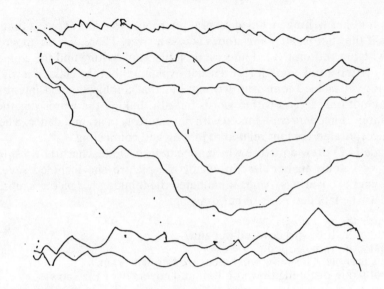

Figure 6.2   'I'm writing'

skills to make their own marks convey the message in a way which re-
sembles convention. This mastery of the power and importance of the
message overrides the capacity to reproduce the conventions of *form*.
Shaun (4:3) disliked and avoided writing; he preferred to be outdoors
involved in more vigorous and energetic activity. On one occasion, he
wanted to go down to the school office to photocopy some of his drawings.
It was a Monday morning and inconvenient for the school clerk involved in
the usual start-of-the-week administration. Children from the nursery were
in the habit of going to the school office, taking with them a note from the
teacher to show that they were on 'official business'. Shaun pestered to go
to the office; his photocopies were essential and he could not wait. He tried
to persuade each member of staff to let him go. Finally the teacher said,
'Shaun, you haven't got a note to say you can go. I can't let you go this
morning, especially without a note, and it's so busy in the office this morning.' Undaunted, Shaun wrote his own note, in his own way (Figure 6.4).
He returned with it to the teacher: 'That says: "boys can go down to the
office",' he said, confidently pressing the note into his teacher's hand, 'so
can I go now?' The teacher endorsed the note with a translation for the
clerk and agreed that he could go later in the morning when the clerk was
less busy. Shaun was satisfied. His knowledge about writing, its power and
his tenacity had won the day. His appreciation of *content* and *meaning*
served to overcome, for the moment, his struggle with aspects of *form*.

Writing as representation
When young children understand that they can make a mark or series of
marks which means *them* they have made an important discovery – and it *is*
a discovery. At this point, children's autographs begin to appear on every

Figure 6.3 'This is writing'

Shaun

that says "boys can go down to the office."

Figure 6.4 'That says "boys can go down to the office" '

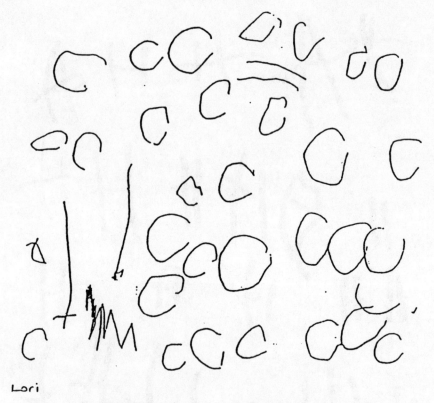

Lori

Figure 6.5 'It's the bit of "Lori" I can't get'

picture and painting, regardless of whether an adult has already written it for them. They write the beginnings of their name *because they can*.

Lori (3:9) produced a piece of writing which at first glance seems to be an attempt to represent the letter *c* (Figure 6.5). But Lori volunteered the real purpose of her writing. 'It's the bit of Lori I can't get.' Perhaps Lori was practising hard, self-motivated, to represent the oval which made the *o* in Lori. She knew it should close but couldn't quite manage to get her hand to do what she wanted. Those adults who remember learning to write might recall the frustration of trying to get the *o* to join up neatly without beginning and end points crossing over.

Stuart was 3 years old when he began nursery. He tended to point and use single words when he wanted to draw attention to something. Writing was apparently new to him. He was acutely aware of his world, noticing minute details in pictures in books and around the nursery, both indoors and outdoors. He was constantly on the move, exploring, investigating and discovering. Stuart's own markmaking was at an early stage, but he seemed to understand that writing had some meaning and could be used to represent things and convey messages. After seeing a notice about story books on the quiet-room door, Stuart did some of his own writing (Figure 6.6). This, he said, was 'writing a door'.

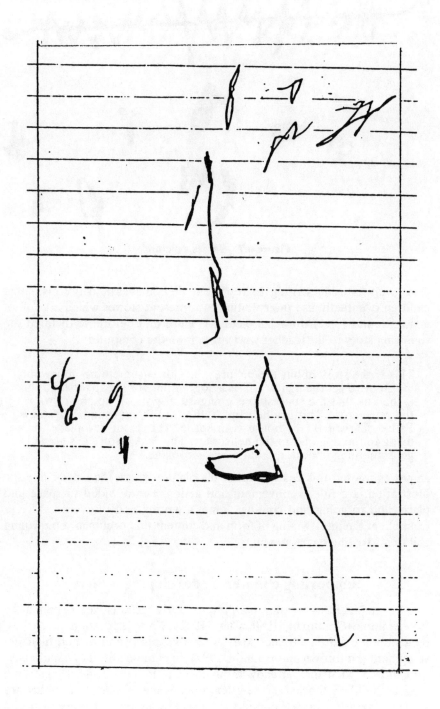

Figure 6.6 'Writing a door'

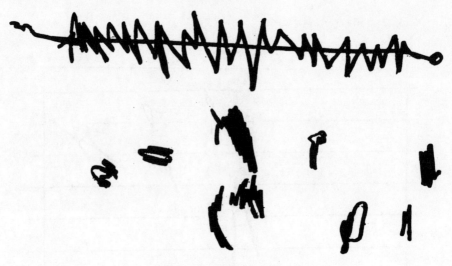

Figure 6.7 'James's picture'

As well as using writing to represent their names and objects, some children eventually use their writing to represent stories which are full of action. James (3:11) drew his picture (Figure 6.7) before he dictated the following story to his teacher who wrote it on the computer:

> *James's picture*
> This is the story about the picture . . . This is something important, it's going to get the lights. This is a dog waiting for the spaceship. This is the line that the spaceship is going on. It goes all up and down all the way across. This is a helicopter, they are flying round. This bit is Father Christmas, his house is in space. This is an aeroplane, he's flying to the dog and to the helicopter. This is Airwolf, he's going to get something important, that other aeroplane.

James composed this description of his picture where the words, like the illustration, are full of movement and action. He attended to space and place, and to going and coming. James's writing and drawing is a clear example of the intertwining of form and content that occurs in some young children's writing development.

Supporting children as developing writers

The development of writing in children's early years is well documented (for example Goodman, 1980; Clay, 1972). Early education at its best builds upon children's home experiences to support and extend their development (Nutbrown and Hannon, 1997). In planning literacy experiences for children, what they already know needs to be taken into account and used as building blocks for new learning. Some 3- and 4-year-olds are already interested in reading and are capable, motivated users of books when they first attend a nursery or playgroup. Others have yet to develop an understanding of how books work and experience the pleasure of listening to stories and sharing books. Similarly, some children know a lot about writing and see themselves as writers whilst others will need support and opportunities to begin to develop as writers.

The role of the professional educator is a key to ensuring that all children are given the teaching they need to fulfil their own potential in developing literacy and to become confident and capable readers and writers. Working with children and parents according to their own stages of understanding and according to their individual needs and interests must be a part of developing early literacy. Professional educators need to be aware of, value and use their important skills and be able to share these with parents. They also need time and professional development opportunities to support them in this aspect of their teaching role.

Because literacy is so important, no time should be lost in developing and extending children's interests and skills in literacy. Talking with parents and finding out what experiences of literacy a child has had in their earliest years at home will help in planning and extending children's opportunities in their first group setting, be it playgroup, nursery or school.

Reading and writing are skills for living, providing the user with a means of access to information and an effective means of communication with others. The power of literacy should never be underestimated. Children need to begin to acquire the invaluable skills, knowledge and understanding about literacy, and appreciate the pleasures of reading and writing from an early age. It is a partnership between all involved with the child (at home and at school), which will maximise opportunity for children's early literacy development.

How can parents support children's literacy development?
There has been increased involvement of parents in children's education generally in recent years and in reading in particular. There is a diversity of ways in which parents are now involved and research has led to some agreement on the need to work with parents (Griffiths and Edmonds, 1986; Lujan, Stolworthy and Wooden, 1986; Winter and Rouse, 1990; Nutbrown and Hannon, 1997).

Some parents involve themselves in their child's literacy development well before the child begins school, demonstrating that parents can play a key role in supporting and promoting their children's literacy development. Parents on a course focusing on young children's learning and development were asked to talk about the things they did which helped to focus children's attention on literacy and to develop their learning. These are some of the things they said they did with their children:

- Pointing out signs when on the bus and signs in shop windows.
- Writing invitations to a party.
- Looking at the labels on tins; naming the soup, spaghetti, other packages.

- Playing the part of a character in the book after reading it together.
- Looking at books, describing pictures, saying which is a favourite and why.
- Putting an alphabet poster on their bedroom wall, looking at letters and saying them.
- Making words from alphabet spaghetti at tea time!
- Choosing books together in the library.

Parents on the same course talked about their ideas and experiences in helping to support their children's literacy development. They recalled doing different things at home with their young children:

> 'She likes writing her own cheques, sending them for bills!'
> 'We read catalogues, she helps to fill in the form for the order!'
> 'I'm always reading adverts on TV, and names that go up at the end of *Neighbours.*'

Perhaps one of the most significant comments came from the parent who said, 'I suppose I do help her to learn, but it's all sort of, natural. I don't think, "this is helping her to learn", I just do it. It's part of life isn't it – reading and writing!'

Weinberger (1996), reporting a study of parents' contributions to children's early literacy development, presents a similar list of activities drawn from examples given by parents she interviewed.

The Raising Early Achievement in Literacy (REAL) Project (Nutbrown and Hannon, 1997) has developed and described four important roles parents might play in supporting their children's literacy development:

- providing literacy *opportunities;*
- showing *recognition* of literacy achievements;
- *interaction* with children around literacy;
- being a *model* of a literacy user.

Parents who are aware of and have some knowledge about early literacy development are in a better position to enhance further the things they often do naturally. They can then enjoy, value and support their young children's literacy development.

How can early education settings support children as developing writers?
Earlier in this chapter, a framework for developing emergent literacy was discussed (Figure 6.1). Early-childhood educators might refer to the framework of *model, provide, observe, interact, intervene* and *evaluate* to develop their own strategies for working with young developing writers and readers.

Children's early markmaking, whatever the stage of accuracy or representation, needs to be encouraged and developed. Early marks and the beginnings of writing included in this chapter form the basis of writing in the conventional form as we know it. To write all the letters in the English alphabet, children need to be able to represent straight and diagonal lines, circles and arcs, to connect marks together and to place marks inside and outside enclosing marks. The early writing and drawing of young children includes much of this repertoire, and alongside the marks develops an understanding of writing, the gradual development of a writing system, increased control and repetition of letters, symbols and words hand-in-hand with experimentation. Young children have the capability to develop all the marks they need to write and, with the support of professional educators following an appropriate teaching framework such as that given in Figure 6.1, they can develop as competent writers. Simultaneously, they need opportunities to forge the words they need and experiences which provide them with something to say when they write. *Content* and *form* of children's writing, nourished in parallel, are important factors in early literacy education. Children need opportunities to practise signs and symbols, good models to understand conventions and purposes, and knowledgeable educators who are well placed to time and tune their interventions to children's current learning needs.

This chapter has focused on the place of *form* and *content* in children's development as writers and readers. Essential to this development is their experience of stories. The importance of stories in children's learning has been discussed by many (e.g. Waterland, 1985; Bennett, 1991; Meek, 1988), all of whom acknowledge that children become readers in the fullest sense of the word when what they read is wide-ranging. Chapter 7 considers the place of stories in children's learning, not just as material for learning to read but as nourishment for their minds.

7
NOURISHING CHILDREN'S THINKING THROUGH STORIES

Stories are fundamental to human experience, and stories experienced in early childhood can extend children's thinking, foster new knowledge, and validate their emotions. This chapter illuminates the importance of fiction in early education and demonstrates the potential of story in fostering children's development and learning. Many examples of early fiction illustrate their important role in developing children's thinking, behaviour, attitudes and beliefs.

Two aspects of narrative in early education will be considered:

1. *Quality in children's literature*, because it is important to ensure that the best of literature is available to children.
2. *Stories as teachers*, because stories contain a wealth of information and stimulus from which children can learn much more than the mechanics of learning to read.

The chapter concludes with a list of stories which can be used as 'nourishment for thinking' to support the ideas developed throughout this chapter.

Quality in children's literature

It is difficult to talk about 'quality' books for children without taking some time to define, however inadequately, what might be meant by this term. One possible interpretation of the term 'quality' in this context could be that books should be neither racist or sexist, should be well illustrated, and well written. Directly the problem of defining quality is compounded. Who decides what is 'well illustrated'? Who decides what is 'good writing' for children? To some extent, these are matters of personal opinion. Some books preferred by children, and considered to be 'good' may well represent 'bad taste' for their parents or teachers! Because of this dilemma of quality, and because books should maximise opportunities for children, the choices teachers make when they select books for their classrooms, and when they read stories to children, are crucially important. Children's literature now offers more choice than ever before, and teachers need to ensure breadth of choice and range of books in their classrooms so that children are not restricted to a narrow view of literature, written language and ideas. Those educators who work with children under 5 in a wide variety of settings have a responsibility to provide a wide range of literature for children to share, learn from and enjoy. To do otherwise would be to deny children opportunities in their early encounters with the written word. It is not acceptable only to provide books purchased from jumble sales or car boot sales. Books are a fundamental tool for learning in early education and as such should not be selected from a limited range of 'cast-offs' but from the widest range of currently published titles.

Quality in children's books is more than promoting equal opportunities and positive images of people from ethnic minorities, of male and female and of different abilities. Quality is much more than skilful and compelling illustrations. It is more than poetic and memorable turns of phrase and a story line which absorbs young readers. Children's books need to include all of these things and more. Children need books which nourish their minds and their emotions, because quality is about feelings as well as thought and knowledge. Many books can help to support as well as challenge children's emotional development, reflecting and affirming their feelings, challenging their thinking and presenting characters who experience different emotions of fear, sadness, excitement, love and disappointment.

Victor Watson (1992, p. 1) challenges readers to define what we mean by children's literature, arguing that the very idea of a category of literature called 'children's' is an 'uncertain concept.' It is important that educators reflect on what they mean by a 'good book' and children also need the freedom and the opportunities to decide what makes a 'good book' for them. For children to begin to develop their own views of quality in the literature they read, they need to experience the most wonderful, the most magical, and the most entrancing literature available. Books can illuminate for children parts of life which are difficult, sad, lonely, exciting, strange, challenging and frightening. Books can show the importance of being fair, stimulate thinking about equality and immerse children in different worlds – both connected and unassociated with their own. Stories can be shared between children and professional educators in group settings and between children and their families at home. Books are not just an instrument for learning about words and happenings but can be an essential part of a loving and intimate experience shared by children and adults.

Children can develop discerning qualities and the ability to decide and articulate what they feel is 'a good book' if given the opportunity to share stories, to hold on to books, and to lose themselves in the pages of a mystery, a fantasy, a thriller, which they feel is just for them.

In 1990, the National Curriculum Programmes of Study for English stated that:

> Reading should include picture books, nursery rhymes, poems, folk tales, myths, legends and other literature which takes account of pupil's linguistic competences and backgrounds. Both boys and girls should experience a wide range of children's literature . . . Pupils should

encounter an environment in which they are surrounded by books and other reading material presented in an attractive and inviting way.

(DES, 1990b, p. 29, para. 3)

In 1996, *Desirable Outcomes* stated that:

Children enjoy books and handle them carefully, understanding how they are organised. They know that words and pictures carry meaning and that, in English, print is read from left to right and from top to bottom.

(DfEE, 1996, p. 3)

Teachers have a responsibility to ensure that literature used by children in school (books which they read for themselves and those which are read to them) is wide-ranging, of high quality and helps to make readers and thinkers flourish.

The books which children encounter in classrooms and nurseries, play-groups and at home, the books which adults share with children at special times, must be books which light in children that flame of the love of zliterature which will burn and burn throughout the whole of their lives. Books can spark that passion in children, and adults responsible for children's learning need to find ways to make this possible – their agenda must include not only the development of children as readers, but as lovers of stories and active participants in the most human of experiences. Sharing stories in the early years of childhood is not just about learning to read, it is about relationships: both between adults and children as they read together, and between children and those characters they meet in the text. Children's literature can support the development of children's language, help them to listen attentively, to talk about interesting things and meaningful content. Experience of sharing stories can stimulate children to create their own versions of the familiar and favourite stories they read and hear.

What are the best books for children?
We say that early education should provide the best of literature for children, but it is not so easy to define what is the 'best'. Quality can be very much a question of personal preference. It could even be said that quality, like beauty, is in the eye of the beholder. Reading a book, or sharing a story, is often a personal encounter – a book which one child loves and enjoys over and over again will be firmly rejected by another. Those who work with young children do not simply need a list of good books to use with children. They need to be able to decide *why* they select certain books for children to explore, *why* they read particular stories, *why* they tend to shun others. For example, *Where the Wild Things Are* (Sendak, 1967) is a humorous and exciting fantasy for some children whilst others find it a terrifying horror story they wish to avoid; the monster's terrible eyes and gnashing teeth are just too much for some young hearts! Such books are still important to children's experiences, because children bring their own experiences, ideas, thoughts and feelings to the books they read, and books too bring ideas, experiences, information and emotions to the children who

read them. When children's own experiences connect in some way to those contained within a story, a match of meaning can occur. Such a match between that which children find important and the stories they read and hear makes the crucial difference between simply hearing a story and really listening with absorbed intent and making it part of their thinking.

Some characteristics of 'good books' can be considered fundamental to children's early literacy experiences. Meek (1988) writes of the 'intertextuality' and the 'multiconsciousness' of books which contain much more than words. There may be two or more stories, different layers of meaning, illustration, timing, one story being conveyed through the text and another, or an embellishment of this story, continuing in the illustrations. Early childhood educators need to develop their own criteria for choosing books for children which maximise opportunities for children to develop their language, literacy and understanding of the world. Criteria will include: the quality of production, illustration, style of language, opportunities for developing particular understandings of text (such as phonological awareness, punctuation, genre), content, and (it must be said) the pleasure they offer the reader.

Books can convey powerful images and messages to young children, so the books they are offered need to be chosen carefully. The following books have been examined to see what they might offer in terms of a literacy experience which holds the potential to children's developing knowledge, ideas, thoughts and emotions.

The Tooth Ball (Pearce, 1987) tells the story of Timmy, a young boy who is sad, shy and without friends. His wobbly tooth falls out. He wraps it first in some gold foil which comes from his grandmother's birthday chocolates. Gradually further layers are added, silver foil, a leaf, Christmas paper, writing paper, brown paper, computer paper. The ball gets bigger as layers of wrapping are added, but it also gets lighter. As the tale progresses, Timmy meets another boy who helps him to put more layers of wrapping on the 'tooth ball', an old sock, kitchen paper, newspaper, wallpaper, a duster, cotton wool, a tea towel, an old woolly hat, a table cloth, a pillow case, a sack, and finally: 'It got bigger and bigger – and lighter and lighter, too, in a most surprising way. They had to wrap it in garden-netting so that Timmy could wind his fingers in it firmly, to stop the toothball from bouncing away.' The two boys take the tooth ball to the park and meet several children who become new friends.

This is a book about relationships, burning heartfelt desire for friends and a grandmother's love. It is (perhaps) a fantasy with a happy ending, but with another ingredient. A central theme is the 'covering' which is described in detail and with imagination. This story can stimulate further learning experiences and act as a starting point for work on coverings and wrappings as well as discussions about friends and loneliness. After telling this story to her class of 5-year-olds, a teacher introduced some work on wrapping and packaging. Using different types of wrapping material, including paper, fabrics, plastics, children began to create their own multilayered balls. Children learned that each time a layer goes on, the size of their ball increased, but also recorded that the weight increased too. Children recorded the type and size of the layering material, and the increasing weight of their layered balls. Working in small groups they discussed, experimented, hypothesised and tried out different ideas. Later they tested their products for durability, seeing how long they would stay intact when used outdoors for throwing, rolling and bouncing. These absorbing and worthwhile activities arose from a single story experience, the creative thinking of their teacher, and the collaborative involvement of the children. The work contained several links to subject areas in the National Curriculum including English, Mathematics, Science and Technology as well as the collaborative work and recording processes which were transferable: attitudes, aptitudes and skills, important in all areas of learning.

A Book of Boxes (Mason, 1989) demonstrates a perfection in the craft of colour and imagination of children's publishing, concealing surprises in the 'boxes' contained on each page. It is a book full of surprise. A nursery nurse was sharing this book with two 4-year-olds. It was the first time they had seen *A Book of Boxes* and the children explored each page with the adult, talking about experiences of which the boxes and their contents reminded them. The two children were keen to see what was inside the different boxes as they turned each page. Later that day one of the children brought a box to the nursery nurse. She offered it to her and said, with a broad smile, 'What's inside this one?' The adult knelt down to open the box. Inside she found six books. The little girl laughed and said 'It's a box of bookses!' She understood that things the wrong way around might be funny, combined it with her experience of the book and made her own joke, reversing the book title to name the object she had created. Both the book and the child's subsequent 'box of bookses' relate to ideas of 'insideness'.

A Dark, Dark Tale (Brown, 1983) is a long-standing testimony to the power of illustration and the economy of words; the cat receives no mention in the text, but is a main character and features frequently in the illustrations. The enchantment of repetition and the expectation in this book is known and enjoyed by everyone who turns the pages:

> Once upon a time there was a dark, dark moor.
> On the moor there was a dark, dark wood.
> In the wood there was a dark, dark house.
> At the front of the house there was a dark, dark door.
> Behind the door there was a dark, dark hall.
> In the hall there were some dark, dark stairs.
> Up the stairs there was a dark, dark passage.
> Across the passage was a dark, dark curtain.
> Behind the curtain was a dark, dark room.
> In the room was a dark, dark cupboard.
> In the cupboard was a dark, dark box.
> And in the box there was . . . A MOUSE!

After hearing this story many, many times both at home and at nursery, Annie (3:7) wrote her own version of the book. She used four sheets of paper fixed together with staples. On each page she drew an oval. She brought the book to her teacher who wrote Annie's words on each page:

Front cover	'Dark Book' 'by Annie'
Page 1	'Dark house'
Page 2	'Dark mouse'
Page 3	'Dark cat'
Back cover	'finished!'

This example of a young child's book-making shows how children who are absorbed by certain stories and ideas can extend these ideas further when there is match between their ideas and new ones. Resources and information need to be offered to them, and adults need to be 'tuned in' to extend and support children's efforts and interests.

These books (and many hundreds more) all have their own distinct qualities. They each offer something particularly special to younger and older readers. They are 'multilayered' (Waterland, 1992). Children benefit from seeing, handling, and owning books like these. They need to talk about such books and hear the stories read by their adults at home and in group provision. They need the experience of sharing stories and books with people who share a passion for story and of literature. Books and stories have a prime place in any effective early education curriculum, and can provide and complement lasting experiences for children.

As well as the written story, the tradition of oral storytelling where tales contain compelling and memorable themes and motifs which sustain both younger and older listeners are important experiences for developing children's sense of 'story'. Listeners bring their own experiences to the story just as the storyteller brings experiences of the story to them.

The 'Story of the Tailor'[1] tells of a tailor who acquired a large length of cloth of a quality he had never worked with before. The tailor proudly made a fine long overcoat which he wore until it was all worn through. Unable to bring himself to throw the cloth away he remade the overcoat into a jacket ('for there was still some good cloth in the overcoat'). Over time the jacket wore out and so the tailor made a waistcoat out of the good cloth which was not so worn and still had some quality left in it. The waistcoat in its time was made into a cap, the cap into a tie. Finally, when the large piece of cloth had been made into garments reducing in size each time, the tailor realised that his tie of the fine cloth was truly worn out. But there was one tiny piece of the tie which was not so worn and the tailor made the smallest thing he could, a button 'the finest he ever had'.

Alongside the compelling style of the storyteller (lost here in the condensed, written version) are two main themes: the first of decreasing size, and the second of the pride and pleasure of the craftsman. The first theme supports mathematical ideas of size and sequence, and the second bears a message about feelings of pride and pleasure in creating and owning something beautiful, and never really wanting to part with it. Such themes recur in many stories and can provide a link with children's schematic interests in 'something inside something inside something'. Storytelling is an important part of many cultures and a way of passing on the history, laws and traditions of a people. The storytelling tradition is important to Native Americans who, in parts of Utah, Arizona, Colorado and New Mexico, produce the 'storytellers' – clay models of storytelling dolls – figures with mouths open (telling a story) and many children sitting on their knees, at their feet, leaning over their shoulders. Traditional tales of the tribe are passed on through stories to the youngest children and stories of traditions and history are told and retold through generations.[2] Traditional tales are often full of pattern, repetition, information and experience which are intended to equip the listener with guidance for living.

Picture books and pop-up books

Many books include attractive features of illustration and movable parts. A number of stories where illustration is strongly schematic and the text tells a different story are of interest to children. For example, some books attract children because of their compelling mastery of paper technology, as in *The Wheels on the Bus* (Zelinsky, 1990) and *The Magic Window* (Nister, 1981). These can stimulate dynamic exchanges between children and adults, and adults need to develop finely tuned skills of observation so that they can be alert to those things which children find important in the books they read.

Picture books and books which contain examples of skilful paper engineering can prompt children to design and create their own books, including features such as illustrations and flaps which lift, as in books like *Where's Spot?* (Hill, 1980), and surprises in pockets such as the letters in *The Jolly Postman* (Ahlberg and Ahlberg, 1986) and the variety of unexpected delight in *A Book of Boxes* (Mason, 1989). Six-year-old Josie created her own version of *The Jolly Postman*. She stapled sheets of paper together and stuck an envelope on each facing page. Over a week, she wrote various letters to the characters in her book, illustrated the pages and made up rhymes to link the letters together as the pages were turned.

Teaching through stories

Children can learn many things through stories. Parents, teachers and other early-childhood educators often seek out a book which they hope will help a child through difficult or challenging times in their lives. *I'll Always Love You* (Wilhelm, 1985) is the story of a small boy and his dog, whom he loves very much. When the dog grows old and dies, the boy's sadness is experienced by all who read this story. *Ben's Baby* (Foreman, 1989) tells of the events and experiences of changes in the life of a little boy whose mother is expecting a second child. Some books convey images and messages about feelings, about the world, about social etiquette and about relationships. Many books written for children portray powerful messages through graphic as well as textual images. In *Rosie's Walk* (Hutchins, 1969) the main characters are Rosie, the hen and the fox. There are 32 words of text in which there is no mention of the fox, but without the fox in the illustrations, *Rosie's Walk* would have been a quite different story. The important interplay between text and illustration is described by Meek (1988) who relates her interaction with a child reading *Rosie's Walk,* and the duality of meaning conveyed through words and pictures.

Earlier chapters have discussed aspects of the form and content of children's thinking. Here stories are considered as a source of rich nourishment for children's developing and lively minds and as such an indispensible resource for teaching. Children's patterns of learning can be enriched by many of the themes which run through stories. Many stories have a number of different themes in common. 'Structures' or 'sub-themes' which lie beneath the content of stories can be identified. Ideas of 'space and place' are important in children's stories (Watson 1992) (p. 11). Watson draws attention to the substructures in *Tom's Midnight Garden* (Pearce, 1958), which is 'full of openings – doors, windows, gaps in hedges' (p. 23). Similarly, *Alice's Adventures in Wonderland* (Carroll, 1865) and *Through the Looking Glass and What Alice Found There* (Carroll, 1871) is a labyrinth of changing size, topsy-turvey, back-to-front and upside-down experiences.

Such underlying structures, themes such as 'insideness', 'up and down', 'rotation and roundness' and 'journeys' are prevalent in children's literature and the following examples illustrate how some children might respond to such story experiences.

'Insideness' in stories

Young children, at different times in their lives, seem to be interested in ideas and experiences of being inside or putting things inside. Being inside, hiding, wrapping things, hiding objects are all part of this apparently compulsive behaviour of young children. Many stories in different ways nourish the theme of insideness. Whilst the form of thinking – 'insideness' – is common in all of the following stories, the variety of content is wide and such stories can therefore be used to stimulate and extend children's ideas and knowledge. As such they are an important teaching resource.

Inside – inside – inside

The development of mathematical concepts of decreasing size can be fostered with stories which tell of an object or objects inside other objects which are themselves inside something else. This idea is the literary equivalent of the Russian Doll which opens to reveal a smaller doll, which also opens to reveal another doll and so on until finally a wee small doll is found inside the penultimate tiny doll. Stories like Ruth Brown's *A Dark, Dark Tale* (see earlier), *Funny Bones* (Ahlberg and Ahlberg, 1982) and Vyanne Samuels's *Boxed In* (1991) fit into this category.

This pattern of thinking is part of the same interest which prompts older children, at the point where they become aware of a larger world and their place in it, to augment their home address by adding, for example: 'London, England, Great Britain, Europe, The World, The Solar System,

The Milky Way, The Universe, Infinity'. Even Professors of Education admit to inscribing their school books in this way. Carr, tells of his discovery of a school book written when he was 13:

> A few years ago while clearing out some books from my mother's attic, I came across an old school history textbook. I turned the flyleaf and read what I had written there.
>
> Wilfred Carr
> 97 Beresford Street
> Moss Side
> Manchester
> Lancashire
> England
> Great Britain
> United Kingdom
> Europe
> The World
> Solar System
> The Universe
>
> This kind of primitive cosmology was not uncommon in 1957 and it is probably still a popular means for children to secure themselves against their initial lack of placement by locating themselves in a reality that is familiar and knowable.
>
> (Carr, 1995, p. 18)

And the idea of 'one's place' is attractive to novelists too, for the address of Abhijit Das in the novel *A Strange and Sublime Address* is:

> 17 Vivekananda Road
> Calcutta (South)
> West Bengal
> India
> Asia
> Earth
> The Solar System
> The Universe
>
> (Chauduri, 1998)

One enclosure – many things inside

Other ideas of insideness which attract children to the concept of 'fitting in' are the ideas of a single enclosure, for example, a house, a bag, a box, which contains an increasing number of things. This is like the carpet bag carried by Mary Poppins, out of which come all manner of objects, large and small, which in reality are far too large to fit inside the bag. Similarly, *A Witch Got on at Paddington Station* (Sheldon and Smith, 1991) tells of a happy witch who gets on a crowded bus on a rainy day. In a tussle with the grumpy conductor her bag breaks and, to the delight of the passengers, out pour its fantastic contents, filling the bus:

> There was a blue moon. There were pink stars.
> There was one fountain. There were two toucans.
> There were three parrots. There were four kittens.
> There were five garden gnomes.

One Snowy Night (Butterworth, 1991) tells the story of a park keeper who is snug and warm in his house on a cold, snowy, winter night. One by one the animals living in the park arrive and ask to be let in to stay the night away from the winter elements. Percy eventually ends up with a squirrel, two rabbits, a fox, a badger, a hedgehog and some mice in his bed. Eventually the animals find other places to snuggle inside: a dressing-gown pocket, a coat pocket, a drawer, a woolly hat and some slippers.

Three-year-old Shelley, having been told this story at home, represented the story in two ways. First, she hid her toy mouse in her father's slipper. When the mouse was discovered she said, 'He was hiding because it was snowy.' Secondly, she drew a rectangle with several ovals inside it and one outside it. She said, 'It's the house and the animals inside but the mole is outside.' She had selected from the story some parts which had meaning for her, and later represented them, first through action, and second through drawing. Her language also matched what she did when she used words like *hiding* and *inside*.

Four-year-old Alistair was retelling his favourite story, *Dinner Time* (Pienkowski, 1980) in which various animals swallow another in turn: a fly, frog, vulture, gorilla, tiger, crocodile and a shark. Alistair mimicked the voices of each animal as he repeated the words in the story, 'I'm going to eat you for my dinner.' Later, playing with a set of zoo animals Alistair re-enacted the story. 'Speaking' for each animal in turn he selected a set of animals ranging from a tiny rabbit to a large elephant. He told the teacher, 'They have to eat the one smaller than them because otherwise it won't fit inside.'

Stories which repeat an idea or a phrase help children in their striving to place some 'order' on their thoughts and on their world. Repetition and patterned texts help children to predict what might come next and to actively engage in storymaking.

Traditional stories based on the theme of insideness include the song of the old woman who swallowed a fly, illustrated in *Fancy That!* (Pienkowski, 1986), 'The House that Jack Built', 'Peter and the Wolf' and 'The Old Woman who Lived in a Shoe'.

Types of enclosure

Stories like *My Presents* (Campbell, 1988), *Dear Zoo* (Campbell, 1984), *The Jolly Postman* (Ahlberg and Ahlberg, 1986) and traditional tales such as 'The Three Little Pigs' also contain themes about different types of enclosure. Many stories include ideas of 'gobbling up', for example: 'Little Red Riding Hood', 'The Three Billy Goats Gruff', and Aesop's fable of 'The Wolf and his Shadow'. Others tell of deep enclosing forests as in 'The Sleeping Beauty'. Similarly the Bible story of 'Jonah and the Whale' tells of Jonah who is swallowed by a large whale and spends three days and nights inside the whale and is eventually spat out onto land. Another Old Testament story of Joseph, made popular through the musical show *Joseph and the Amazing Technicolor Dreamcoat*, contains several enclosures. Williams retells this tale in *Joseph and his Magnificent Coat of Many Colours* (Williams, 1990) where Joseph experiences many types of enclosure: his magnificent coat, a deep pit and a prison cell.

One enclosure – many uses

Jack's Basket (Catley, 1989), written in rhyme, tells of different uses, over the passage of time, for Jack's baby basket; his bed for the first few months, a wool basket, a pretend car or boat, a picnic basket, a laundry basket, something to gather apples in from the tree in the garden and, finally, battered and worn, it becomes a home for mice in the garden shed. In *Fur* (Mark and Voake, 1986) a cat makes a series of nests ready to give birth to her kittens; she uses a hat, a basket in a cupboard and a skirt, but finally the hat is filled with 'fur' and the kittens have arrived. Maya (4:6), familiar with this story, made 'a hat' from clay, explaining to her mother: 'I did this hat, and tomorrow there will be kittens but they haven't been born from the mummy cat yet.' As children develop some understanding of time, they realise that there are times when there is a need to wait before things happen. Maya knew that there was some waiting involved when a cat has kittens, and here the making of the hat portrayed her understanding.

Coverings

The theme of 'coverings' includes many avenues for exploration and representation: several covers on top of one another, making coverings, disguise and dressing up. Several stories already mentioned enrich these ideas. Many stories have several interrelated ideas which will connect in different ways with children's interests and imaginations.

The Hans Anderson tale of 'The Emperor's New Clothes' is a story which can appeal to children who understand about clothing and covering (and of being tricked) (Anderson, 1992). Children who can imagine the scene may find it funny that so many people were too stupid to admit that the Emperor was not wearing any clothes. A more contemporary story, *Mr Nick's Knitting* (Wild and Huxley, 1990) has as a central theme the making of a blanket from knitted squares. This story describes the deep feelings of real and loving friendship and the need of a friend to give something truly unique to a person who is a very special friend.

Children love to dress up and pretend to be a different person. They delight in adopting and creating roles where they are different from their daily lives – more powerful, more exotic, perhaps more feeble than they see themselves to be. Stories of dressing up or changing appearances through disguise can be used to nourish and extend children's ideas of coverings, and of being wrapped inside as well as the fear and excitement of being different and exploring new identities. Two animal stories describe the potential of looking different by taking on a different covering. *Elmer* (McKee, 1989) tells of a multicoloured elephant who covers himself with grey mud so that he looks the same as, and is therefore acceptable to, the rest of the herd. It is a story of difference and of the need to be accepted by one's peers. It shows how effective (and ultimately ineffective) some disguises can be. Accidental disguise, as in *Harry the Dirty Dog* (Zion and Bloy Graham, 1960), also shows reactions to those who look different.

For children, the idea of disguise is quite intriguing. After telling both *Elmer* and *Harry the Dirty Dog* to a group of 4-year-olds, their teacher noted how a small group continued the theme of coverings from the stories into their play that afternoon. The children draped themselves with fabric lengths from the dressing-up wardrobe, approached other children, disguised their voices and asked children to guess who they were or declared that they were a different character. The teacher suggested to the children that they might improve their disguise by making masks. Materials were assembled and the interested children worked with their teachers to make masks of different characters. They later enjoyed the whole idea of surprising and creating puzzlement amongst their friends and parents who saw them wearing their masks and disguises.

Up and down

Many stories include ideas of vertical movement with concepts of increasing height and of problem-solving related to height. The following examples of stories and children's responses to them show the variety of ideas which can be introduced through this theme. Many traditional stories include ideas of height and of conquering height. Jack climbs the beanstalk to encounter the Giant, and achieve wealth and happiness. Rapunzel lets down her long hair for her suitor to climb to meet her.

Illustrators represent variations in height in many different ways. Shirley Hughes's picture book *Up and Up* (1991) tells, in detailed illustrations, the story of a little girl so enthralled with the flight of a bird that she tries to fly. First she makes some wings and launches herself (into an abrupt landing) from the top of a step ladder; then she inflates some balloons and, holding tight onto the strings, she lifts off, only to fall to ground again when the balloons burst. An enormous chocolate egg is delivered to her house, and after eating the contents she seems able to fly; the story proceeds from here with her flight (and the pursuit of many).

This story allows children to tell their own version of events. They can speculate on why she wanted to fly, how else she might have tried, and be asked: 'Can chocolate really make you fly?' They might, as the following example shows, begin to tell their own story in their own way, incorporating their own excitement, fears and anticipations. The following transcript contains the story which one little girl had to tell, starting from her interest in a particular illustration in the book, and building on her ideas about life and that which was important to her. Throughout this exchange the adult tried to reflect the child's own language and ideas back to her without asking new questions that impose an 'adult' agenda on Lucy's story:

Lucy: She's going up, right up to the roof.
Teacher: She's up on top of the roof, she's getting higher.
Lucy: I think she might be in heaven soon.

Teacher: You think she might be in heaven?
Lucy: Well, she's nearly high enough to be in heaven, that's why the people are chasing her.
Teacher: The people are chasing her because they think she's getting as high as heaven?
Lucy: Yes, as high as heaven, they don't want her to go as high as that!
Teacher: They don't want her to go as high as heaven?
Lucy: If you go as high as heaven you get stuck and can't get down. You can get up there but you can't get back. My rabbit did that. Aeroplanes go high but not as high as heaven, so they're OK. I went to my holiday in an aeroplane, but it wasn't in heaven, I went for a long time though.

The picture book *Up and Up* was the trigger for this little girl to tell her own story. Both the book and the reflective language of the teacher enabled the child to tell the story she had formed within her. She had, in her young mind, begun to understand about death and parting and used the explanation that her rabbit has 'gone to heaven', attaching to it her own meaning. To her, going to heaven is not about death, but it *is* about parting because that loved rabbit was stuck in a place and unable to get back to her. The teacher's important interaction here was to enable Lucy to tell her story, not by asking 'why' or 'how' by adding in ideas of her own or by asking new questions, but by creating a space in which the child could tell her story in her own words, with her own ideas.

Many stories include the idea of increasing size, woven into the text along with other concepts. *Titch* (Hutchins, 1972) conveys the feelings and experiences of many children who are always the little one of the family. After seeming always to play a less significant role to everyone else in the story, Titch eventually planted a tiny seed which '. . . grew and grew and grew'. *Jasper's Beanstalk* (Butterworth, 1995) follows the same theme of waiting and growing, and links at the end to the story of Jack and the Beanstalk, enforcing the theme of height and growing. *Alfie Gets in First* (Hughes, 1982) is another story of a little child who needs to solve the problem of his lack of height, featuring trauma of childhood mishaps, the anxiety of adults and eventual resolution. *Jolly Snow* (Hissey, 1992) includes ideas of height and problem-solving; some toy animals who want to play in snow try several ways of making pretend snow indoors. Using a sheet they create a toboggan run:

'Now if we had a slope,' said Rabbit, 'we could whizz down it on the sledge.' . . . Bramwell Brown disappeared into the bedroom and came back pulling a large white sheet. He gave a corner to Jolly. 'Now,' said Bramwell, 'when the others climb on, lift up your end and they should slide all the way down.'

The animals try this but have rather a dubious landing:

'I think we need a softer landing,' said Rabbit, fluffing up his flattened fur and helping Little Bear to his feet. He piled up a heap of cushions against the wall and then all three toys bravely climbed back onto the sheet. 'Ready, steady, go!' they called to Jolly. Up went the sheet. Down went the toys – straight into the heap of cushions . . .

This short extract llustrates ways in which ideas of height, and problem-solving in relation to height, can be introduced or expanded in children's literature, a further resource for teaching.

In *The Teddy Bear Robber* (Beck, 1989) Tom pursues the giant who steals his teddy: 'he slipped down a massive arm, swung on a big iron key and slithered down a mighty leg . . . They came to the Giant's castle. Tom clambered up the steep steps after the Giant . . . higher, and higher, and higher, and higher . . . until they came to a giant door . . .' The words 'higher and higher, and higher and higher' interwoven with illustration, illuminate the scene for young readers and listeners.

Some stories which convey ideas of 'up and down' and of increasing or decreasing height contain plots which require certain knowledge to be fully appreciated. Children who understand the prickliness of a hedgehog can appreciate the humour of being catapulted high into the air after sitting on a hedgehog's sharp spines, as is the fate of *Willoughby Wallaby* (Alborough, 1986). Similarly, children need to understand the concept of displacement to grasp a fuller meaning of the story of 'The Fox and the Grapes' (Aesop).

Rotation and roundness

Many traditional rhymes and jingles include ideas of roundness and rotation, which adults can share with children and which can be sung, changed and acted out; for example, 'Here We Go Round the Mulberry Bush', 'Sally Go Round the Sun', 'Round and Round the Garden'. Stories too can nurture the ideas of movement and action linked to concepts of rotation and roundness, such as *Cupboard Bear* (Alborough, 1989) which includes the idea of rolling and rotation as Bear dreams of a huge ice-cream ball.

Books with moving parts can also contribute to children's developing ideas about rotation. *The Wheels on the Bus* (Zelinsky, 1990) is a feast of movement and colour based on the rhyme and finger song. It includes wheels, and text, which rotate.

Journeys and Journeying

Ideas of journeys and journeying in children's stories often begin with children travelling between different connecting points, for example, their house and their friend's house. Stories about journeying, whether around the house, in a local area or across continents, are of relevance to children who are interested in trajectories (that is, ideas of movement from point 'A' to point 'B' and so on). A theme of journeys and journeying will nourish elements of back-and-forth schema, fuelling children's ideas through fantasy and reality of going and coming. Children's literature contains a wealth of material to support this theme.

In *On the Way Home* (Murphy, 1982), Claire meets various friends who ask how she hurt her knee. This gives her the opportunity to tell a number of quite fantastic stories. Eventually when she gets home she tells her mum what really happened. The characters Claire brings into the story through her own interwoven stories make a simple journey home and a grazed knee into quite an adventure. *Hold Tight, Bear!* (Maris, 1990) describes the walk of some toys into the forest where they have a picnic: 'Over the hills, across the stream, to a meadow near the woods . . . Bear walks under the tall trees, through the cool quiet woods . . .' The passages of text which describe the journey provide for children some of the language of mapping and mapwork. The story also includes the concepts of direction, position, space and place. Such ideas are also found in *The Ball* (Lloyd and Rees, 1991), where the text describes the path of the moving red ball and the illustrations show the bouncing movement, indicating where the ball has been as well as its present position. Some journeying stories have become well-known classics. *Where the Wild Things Are* (Sendak, 1967) and *The Snowman* (Briggs, 1980) tell of two boys who experience fantastic journeys. Are they dreams or are they fantasy? The reader must decide. Maurice Sendak (1967) describes journeying through time and place to take Max to his adventure with the wild things. Max travels in a private boat:

> . . . he sailed off through night and day
> and in and out of weeks
> and almost over a year
> to where the wild things are.

Oi! Get Off Our Train (Burningham, 1991) tells of another bedtime journey where a little boy and his pyjama-case dog travel on their train through fog, heat, wind, marshland, rain, forest and snow rescuing endangered species as they go. *We're Going on a Bear Hunt* (Rosen and Oxenbury, 1989) tells of a journey and an eventful return home revisiting all the landmarks of the outward trip.

Young children who are interested in places and journeying often create their own maps, diagrams and recreations of spaces and places they know. Kirstie was absorbed with ideas of space and place and, in particular, with the idea of getting from one place to another. She used wooden bricks to recreate her own local community environment, labelling various blocks, 'my house', 'Auntie June's house', 'nursery', 'Adam's house'. She used small people to represent different characters and moved them from one place to another. Her words provided a running commentary of her thinking and the action:

Kirstie doll:	I'm going to Auntie June's house.
Mummy doll:	*(Protests)* You can't go on your own.
Kirstie doll:	Yes I can – I won't talk to the wolf.
Mummy doll:	Oh all right – but don't pick flowers in the forest. *(Kirstie walks the doll around her brick world to Adam's house)*

Kirstie doll:	Knock knock – is Adam coming with me? *(Adam doll is brought into the game and Kirstie with Adam doll in one hand and the doll representing herself in the other continues her tale as she moves both dolls around the brick village she has created)*
Kirstie doll:	Shall we go to Auntie June's?
Adam doll:	Oh all right.
Kirstie doll:	We're there now – knock knock *(nothing happens)*
Adam doll:	She's not in.
Kirstie doll:	Well, we can't go in the woods – 'cos the wolf might get us. *(Kirstie walks the dolls around again, humming to herself. She takes them in and out of brick enclosures, through tiny gaps in the bricks and eventually back to her house)*

Kirstie later drew what she called 'my house'. It consisted of four square enclosures and connecting dotted lines. Pointing to appropriate parts of her drawing, Kirstie told her teacher, 'My house, Auntie June's house, Adam's house, nursery', then tracing her finger along the dotted line she said, 'That's the way we go to nursery. We get Adam first, then go through there and along there and down there, past the phone box and to nursery in there.' Kirstie's map showing the way to nursery was created from her knowledge of her local environment, her life experiences, her understanding and experience of stories and her understanding and skill in using symbols to represent things. Her journey may not have been quite as fantastic as those of Max, or the boy who flew with the Snowman, but it was founded in her own experiences and perhaps validated by the many of the stories she had heard.

Stories and Compulsory National Curriculum

The tremendous potential of stories as a resource for teaching has been demonstrated. As well as nourishing more 'traditional' areas of learning as defined in terms of subjects, such as Mathematics, Science, History, Geography and others identified in the National Curriculum, stories can nurture other important elements in children's learning and development often overlooked by those who determine and prescribe national curriculum. For example, *The Stop Watch* (Lloyd and Dale, 1986) is a story which focuses on timing events; it supports concepts of time and timing but is also about competition and the relationship between a brother and sister. Similarly, stories such as *Oi! Get Off Our Train* (Burningham, 1991) can be used to highlight and reinforce effects of environmental damage with human and emotional content as well. Stories are an important resource for helping children to affirm and recognise their emotions.

Children's ways of learning do not change because national policies or prescribed curriculum change. The successful understanding of curriculum content depends upon classroom practice, on teachers' interactions with children, on stimulating and challenging resources and experiences and on pedagogy which holds learners and learning as central. Stories, fully and skilfully explored, are a rich source of curriculum content, which can find a 'match' with young children's minds.

The practice of planning curriculum around stories has been developed by several in recent years resulting in publications which promote, for example, Science, Design and Technology (Creary *et al.*, 1991; Williams, 1991; Design Council, 1992; Nutbrown and Hirst, 1993); History (Cox and Hughes, 1990); and cross-curricular themes and issues, (Development Education Centre, 1991; Emblen and Schmitz, 1991).

Despite pressure to deliver a narrow curriculum programme, those who work with children under the age of statutory schooling still have a curriculum freedom which, whether they work in nursery schools and classes or other forms of provision such as playgroups and crèches, allows them to draw on the richness of the world to provide nourishment for the minds of young children. Teachers working with children in the early stages of Key Stage 1 can take those ideas from the prescribed curriculum which provides for meaningful curriculum content for children, and add to and enrich them according to the various interests and concerns of the children. Despite prescribed criteria for curriculum inspection, there remains a curriculum freedom in teaching children under 5 which means that they can still experience the more 'natural curriculum' mediated through responsive and respectful pedagogy which nourishes young minds.

Young children must not be subjected to an ill-conceived version of a National Curriculum, but a responsibly crafted curriculum attuned to them. A 'natural' early-education curriculum must contain a wealth of stories: myths, legends, traditional stories from many different cultures, stories from children's own local histories and localities, and Greek myths, Aesop's fables, Bible stories and the Anansi stories. Stories told, read, retold and reenacted, become the hidden teachers of young children, open the doors of their minds to the wider world and validate their own inner worlds of storymaking.

Stories as nourishment for thinking

In the following pages books are listed under broad themes which can be related to the different concepts, topics and schemas which have been discussed in this chapter and throughout this book. Such themes can provide profitable curriculum content and stimulate children's interests and imaginations. This illustrates the wide range of content to be drawn from stories to nourish specific threads of children's thinking. The stories are presented here under the themes already discussed in this chapter: insideness, coverings, up and down, rotation and roundness, and journeys and journeying. These lists are by no means comprehensive and are included to exemplify the range and depth of material which stories can offer.

'Insideness'

Inside – inside – inside
Ahlberg, J. and Ahlberg, A. (1980) *Funny Bones*, Picture Lions, London.
Brown, R. (1983) *A Dark, Dark Tale*, Scholastic Publications, London.
Pienkowski, J. (1980) *Dinner Time,* Gallery Five, London.
Pienkowski, J. (1986) *Fancy That!,* Orchard Books, London.
Samuels, V. (1991) *Boxed In*, Red Fox, London.
Traditional tale: 'Peter and the Wolf'.

One enclosure – increasing amount inside
Allan, P. (1989) *Who Sank the Boat?,* Picture Puffin, Harmondsworth.
Burningham, J. (1978) *Mr Gumpy's Outing,* Puffin, Harmondsworth.
Burninghan, J. (1980) *The Shopping Basket*, Jonathan Cape, London.
Butterworth, N. (1991) *One Snowy Night,* Picture Lions, London.
Sheldon, D. and Smith, W. (1991) *A Witch Got on at Paddington Station*, Red Fox, London.
Williams, M. (1988) *Noah's Ark*, Walker Books, London.
Traditional tale: 'The Old Woman Who Lived in a Shoe'.

Types of enclosures
Ahlberg, J. and Ahlberg, A. (1986) *The Jolly Postman or Other People's Letters*, Heinemann, London.
Campbell, R. (1984) *Dear Zoo*, Puffin, Harmondsworth.
Campbell, R. (1988) *My Presents*, Campbell Blackie Books, London.
Hill, E. (1980) *Where's Spot?*, Heinemann, London.
Mark, J. and Voake, C. (1986) *Fur*, Walker Books, London.
Mason, L. (1989) *A Book of Boxes*, Orchard Books, London.
Roffey, M. (1982) *Home Sweet Home*, Piper, London.
Sieveking, A. and Lincoln, F. (1989) *What's Inside?*, Frances Lincoln, London.
Aesop's fable: 'The Fox and the Grapes', in Clarke, M. and Voake, C. (1990) *The Best of Aesop's Fables*, Walker Books, London.
Traditional tale: 'The Three Little Pigs'.

One enclosure, different uses
Catley, A. (1987) *Jack's Basket*, Beaver Books, London.
Prater, J. (1987) *The Gift,* Puffin, Harmondsworth.

Coverings
Anderson, H. C., 'The Emperor's New Clothes', in Ash, N. and Higton, B. (eds) (1992) *Fairy Tales from Hans Anderson – A Classic Illustrated Edition*, Pavilion Books, London.
McKee, D. (1989) *Elmer*, Andersen Press, London.
Pearce, P. (1987) *The Tooth Ball*, Picture Puffins, Harmondsworth.
Wild, M. and Huxley, D. (1990) *Mr Nick's Knitting*, Picture Knight, London.

Zion, G. and Bloy Graham, M. (1960) *Harry the Dirty Dog*, The Bodley Head, London.

Up and down
Alborough, J. (1986) *Willoughby Wallaby*, Walker Books, London.
Butterworth, N. (1995) *Jasper's Beanstalk*.
Dale, P. (1991) *The Elephant Tree*, Walker Books, London.
Edwards, H. and Niland, D. (1982) *There's a Hippopotamus on our Roof Eating Cake!*, Hodder & Stoughton, London.
Hissey, J. (1992) *Jolly Snow*, Random Century, London.
Hughes, S. (1991) *Up and Up*, Red Fox, London.
Hutchins, P. (1972) *Titch*, The Bodley Head, London.
Inkpen, M. (1991) *The Blue Balloon*, Picture Knight, London.
Miko, Y. (1993) *Little Lumpty*, Walker, London.
Aesop's fable: 'The Fox and the Grapes', in Clarke, M. and Voake, C. (1990) *The Best of Aesop's Fables*, Walker Books, London.
Traditional tales: 'Jack and the Beanstalk' and 'Rapunzel'.

Rotation and roundness
Alborough, J. (1989) *Cupboard Bear*, Walker Books, London.

Books with rotating parts
Nister, E. (1981) *The Magic Window*, Harper Collins, Glasgow.
Zelinsky, P. (1990) *The Wheels on the Bus*, Orchard Books, London.

Journeys and journeying
Bayley, N. and Mayne, W. (1981) *The Patchwork Cat*, Jonathan Cape, London.
Beck, I. (1989) *The Teddy Bear Robber*, Doubleday, Toronto.
Briggs, R. (1980) *The Snowman*, Puffin, Harmondsworth.
Burningham, J. (1963) *Borka – The Adventures of a Goose with no Feathers*, Jonathan Cape, London.
Burningham, J. (1991) *Oi! Get Off Our Train*, Red Fox, London.
Cartwright, R. and Kinmonth, P. (1979) *Mr Potter's Pigeon*, Hutchinson Junior Books, London.
Dale, P. (1991) *The Elephant Tree*, Walker Books, London.
Fair, S. (1989) *Barney's Beanstalk*, Macdonald, London.
Flack, M. and Weise, K. (1991) *The Story about Ping*, Random Century, London.
Hughes, S. (1991) *Up and Up*, Red Fox, London.
Hutchins, P. (1969) *Rosie's Walk*, The Bodley Head, London.
Lloyd, D. and Rees, M. (1991) *The Ball*, Walker Books, London.
Lear, E. and Cooper, H. (1991) *The Owl and the Pussycat*, Hamish Hamilton, London.
Maris, R. (1990) *Hold Tight Bear!*, Walker Books, London.

Murphy, J. (1982) *On the Way Home*, Pan Macmillan Children's Books, London.

Pearce, P. (1987) *The Tooth Ball*, Picture Puffins, Harmondsworth.

Prater, J. (1987) *The Gift*, Puffin, Harmondsworth.

Rosen, M. and Oxenbury, H. (1989) *We're Going on a Bear Hunt*, Walker Books, London.

Sendak, M. (1967) *Where the Wild Things Are*, The Bodley Head, London.

Shapur, F. (1991) *The Rainbow Balloon*, Simon & Schuster, London.

Wild, M. and Huxley, D. (1990) *Mr Nick's Knitting*, Picture Knight, London.

Zion, G. and Bloy Graham, M. (1960) *Harry the Dirty Dog*, The Bodley Head, London.

Aesop's fable: 'The Hare and the Tortoise', in Clarke, M. and Voake, C. (1990) *The Best of Aesop's Fables*, Walker Books, London.

Notes

1. I heard Pat Ryan tell the story of the tailor at the Sheffield Early Years Literacy Association Conference, June 1991.

2. More information on this topic can be found in Bahti, M. (1988) *Pueblo Stories and Storytellers*, Treasure Chest Publications, Tucson, Ariz.

Part IV
Implications for early education

8
A CURRICULUM FOR THINKING CHILDREN

The 'spiral curriculum': If one respects the ways of thought of the growing child, if one is courteous enough to translate material into his logical forms and challenging enough to tempt him in advance, then it is possible to introduce him at an early age to the ideas and styles that in later life make an educated man. We might ask, as a criterion for any subject taught in primary school, whether, when fully developed, it is worth an adult's knowing, and whether having known it as a child makes a person a better adult. If the answer to both questions is negative or ambiguous, then the material is cluttering the curriculum.
(Bruner, J. 1960, p. 52)

This chapter will consider the kind of curriculum that young children need in order to develop their thinking, knowing, skills and understandings. Creating respectful curriculum for young children requires (as Bruner asserted almost forty years ago) an examination of what is worth teaching. Meaningful experiences are the essence of a respectful and challenging curriculum.

The debate about the 'gifts' of nature and the 'effects' of nurture have rumbled on through the decades. Those responsible for the education of young children must believe that nurturing young minds can have a positive effect on their learning and development. To subscribe to a theory that asserts that potential understanding and achievement are decided in the womb, rather than developed from the cradle, leads nowhere and guarantees that early education will be ineffective. Nourishment for children's minds, and emotions (as for their bodies), must be matched to need. Such a 'match' of curriculum nourishment must include realistically high expectations held by educators of the children they teach.

Athey (1990) suggests that early intervention, an education that involves parents, professionals and a clear pedagogy, can enhance children's cognitive development. Enhanced knowing, ability and understanding can contribute to enhanced self-esteem and a more grounded holistic development for children. Fundamental to the practices of teaching young children and to the construction of a curriculum to foster their learning are the aims and principles upon which such curriculum rests.

The examples of children's learning and thinking in this book suggest two questions that need to be addressed if curriculum developments in nurseries and other early years group settings are to provide ways for children to develop *as thinkers*. The first, despite official pronouncements on what constitutes an early childhood curriculum, is a perennial question:

● How can professional educators ensure breadth, balance and relevance in the curriculum they offer?

The second question attempts to incorporate understanding of children's *thinking* into provision for their *learning*:

● How can a curriculum for young children nourish children's *forms* of thought with worthwhile and interesting *content*?

Ensuring breadth, balance and relevance in the curriculum

What young children *should* learn has been the subject of continued debate and argument throughout the 1990s. Since the introduction of a National Curriculum for children of statutory school age, the dawn of a mandatory curriculum for children of pre-compulsory school age has been breaking and consultation during 1999 on a 'Foundation Stage' for the National Curriculum brought this a step closer'. Simultaneously, there was emerging a developing curriculum for babies and toddlers. As the demand for more group care of the youngest children grows, so does the debate about what kind of quality it should offer: 'Day care must not just be a safe, clean parking place with good food, fresh air and kind bustling adults. Babies and toddlers must learn to express and exchange emotions, to communicate, and to learn about people, objects, and experiences' (Rouse, 1990, p. 7).

What was interesting about these two developments was that the National Curriculum for 5–16-year-olds seemed to be devised along the lines of setting targets for older children and defining work for younger children on the basis of 'what they will need to know by when', a 'top-down' model of curriculum prescription. Conversely, those working with the youngest, children aged 0–3, were not encumbered by government requirement or targets or anticipated achievement. They were able to work from what they saw babies and toddlers doing, from perspectives of development, from need. They were able to be creative and responsive in the curriculum they developed, moulding and shaping it, in every sense, to fit particular needs of particular children at particular times.

Caught between this creative and responsive approach to curriculum development for children under 3, and the tightly defined skills and subject-based curriculum for children over 5, were those working with children in the 3–5 age range. They were sandwiched between curriculum development opportunities which were creative and open (albeit often under-recognised) and narrow definitions and requirements of what older children should learn.

There was recognition that the 3–5 age range should have a distinct curriculum. Throughout the 1980s and 1990s government documents endorsed the idea of a specialist curriculum for children under 5. The

Education Reform Act 1988 instigated a curriculum for children aged 5–16 designed and defined in terms of subjects and assessed in terms of attainment targets with levels of attainment for each key stage. This curriculum has been the subject of continued controversy, debate and revision since its inception, and changes continue. During the early implementation stages of the National Curriculum, the Rumbold Committee (DES, 1990a), reporting on the quality of educational experience of 3- and 4-year-olds in all settings, considered a curriculum 'framework', based on broad areas of experience and learning opportunities, which together made up a balanced and broad curriculum, was the best way to proceed for young children under 5 years of age. HMI (DES, 1989a) had already set forward this view so far as nursery schools and classes were concerned, and there was some broad consensus about its appropriateness.

Perhaps strangely, what is essentially the official curriculum for children aged 3–5 years finally came about because of funding arrangements initiated by the government in 1996. The document *Desirable Outcomes of Nursery Education* (DfEE, 1996) was not so much a curriculum as a set of criteria for assessment of children or inspection of provision. Government-funded provision for 3–5-year-olds was to be required to demonstrate how it enabled children to meet the stated outcomes in what were termed personal and social development; language and literacy; mathematics; knowledge and understanding of the world; physical development; and creative development. The *Desirable Outcomes* document contained a passing reference to play as a medium for learning and placed clear emphasis on socialising children for school and achievement in literacy and numeracy. The intended progression from pre-compulsory to compulsory education at level 2 of Key Stage 1 was clearly set out (DfEE, 1996, p. 10), as was the purpose of such provision: 'to provide a foundation for later achievement' (p. 1).

Hot on the heels of this narrow definition of children's early achievements came plans for assessment of children on entry to school. *The National Framework of Baseline Assessment* (SCAA, 1996) was introduced in September 1998, requiring all schools to carry out a Baseline Assessment of children within the first half-term of their beginning compulsory schooling (regardless of whether or not the children were, themselves, of compulsory school age). Chapter 9 will consider issues of assessment, but it is sufficient to say here that, within less than a decade, early education in the UK moved from no officially defined, recognised or required *curriculum* to imposed assessment of achievements (often before 5 years of age) at the start of school in literacy, Mathematics and aspects of Personal and Social Development.

Official requirements for providing for young children's learning are generally narrow and often over-specific. Effective educators must focus not just on areas of experience or so-called 'desirable outcomes' but also on ways of extending and linking different strands of knowledge and understanding and experience. Such teaching can give young children opportunities for learning and development that are rich and full and create an experience of early education that is satisfying in holistic terms and reaches beyond official descriptors of required learning and extends the parameters of knowledge. A balanced, broad, relevant and differentiated curriculum is much more than rhetoric. It is a sound philosophy of curriculum entitlement for all children who can be taught and can learn according to their needs and in tune with their potential.

Subjects are one way of categorising elements of knowledge into convenient groupings so that teaching and assessment can be managed and curriculum discussed, but this is not the only way of learning about things and the sometimes constrained compartmentalisation of learning into subjects can be less than helpful in terms of understanding and challenging young children's thinking. The irrelevance of subject-based approaches to teaching young children is ably demonstrated by Hurst and Joseph, who wrote:

> . . . for young children a 'subject-based' approach to a curriculum is inappropriate, as it goes against the ways in which children think and learn. The programmes of study in the present National Curriculum are divided into areas – Art; Geography; English; Mathematics; Physical Education; Science; Information Technology and Design Technology – and this goes against the grain of what we have been saying. On the other hand, the holistic way of learning *is* partly recognised within the National Curriculum. The notion of 'cross-curricular themes, dimensions and skills' subscribes to the fact that bringing different kinds of subject knowledge together can be the most fruitful way of promoting learning, and those practitioners who are involved with carrying out the National Curriculum would do their children a great favour if they made the most of that acknowledgement.
>
> (Hurst and Joseph, 1998, pp. 22–3)

In reality, young children do not think in subjects. Neither do adults. Human beings think in terms of situations, puzzles, problems to be solved, questions to be answered; it is the same for adults and children alike. When children are thinking, talking and applying their existing knowledge, the children attend to the task in hand. Children do not analyse their knowledge in terms of subjects, as the following example illustrates.

A group of children (aged 4:8–4:11) in a reception class were playing with a tray of sand and some small animals. They were creating a story. This story began when one child declared that all the animals had died and needed to be buried. A mass burial of tigers, monkeys, giraffes, elephants, whales, seals, penguins and tigers was arranged. Next the children dug up their animals, having decided they would start again. They made the sand slightly damp, taking care not to add too much water. The children patted the sand to make it flat and then arranged some twigs in a circle to make a forest. Inside the twigs was the forest. The circle represented the 'edge' of the forest. Shells were arranged to represent 'the sea at the edge of the forest'. The group agreed that some of the animals lived 'inside the forest' whilst others lived 'under the sea', so the animals were located in their respective habitats. One child began sprinkling sand over the twigs and said, 'It's snowing, the forest is all covered with snow because it hasn't got a roof on. The animals are covered in snow. They'll die if they freeze to death.' Again, many of the animals died. It was the small animals who suffered this fate for they were 'too small to survive the cold winter'. They were given respectful burials, with due ceremony, in graves of suitably measured size at the centre of the forest. Small memorial notices were written and stuck in the ground to mark the graves.

Educators who watch and interact with children who incorporate all that they know in purposeful play can learn much about those children. They can learn things which focusing on subject knowledge alone would never reveal. These children sustained their work together with sensitive co-operation to be admired. Their story evolved as they were stimulated by the materials provided by the teacher, the stories they had heard, their ideas about dying and burial and their knowledge of the conventions (for example, of marking graves and of the survival of the fittest). Could a teacher contrive such a scenario to such purpose?

Christian Schiller wrote of the difficulty posed by the very term 'curriculum':

> Curriculum is not an attractive word. Whether heard through the ear as a sound, or seen through the eye as a shape on a page, it leaves an impression of something sharp and harsh. It is, of course, a Roman word, unaltered and unassimilated by our native tongue; and this fact no doubt reveals a certain tardiness in finding a native word which says, quite simply and with feeling, 'What we do in school'. Perhaps also it reflects a certain reluctance to think in general terms of all those activities with which children find themselves engaged by our choice as teachers.
>
> And this is not surprising. Curriculum has for long conventionally been used as a collective noun to denote a collection of subjects. But in the field of primary education we are becoming increasingly clear that for young children 'subjects' have little significance.
>
> (Schiller, 1979, p. 3)

The Early Years Curriculum Group advocated breadth of curriculum and illustrated the diversity of learning which is possible through first-hand experience and activity:

> In the early years the child's knowledge is not separated into subject groupings. When children are cooking, for instance, they may be learning about Science, Maths, Health Education, and how to collaborate and share while extending their vocabulary and language skills. Young children learn about 'subjects' through a wide variety of play activities. Play takes many forms, both indoors and outdoors; the skilled observer recognises the significance of these activities and promotes children's understanding and learning. Real objects and materials enable children to explore and extend what they already know and can do. Through a wide range of materials they will be covering many subject areas of the curriculum.
>
> (The Early Years Curriculum Group, 1992, p. 19)

As well as endorsing a curriculum for under-5s made up of areas of experience, the Rumbold Committee and HMI stated the importance of the *processes* of learning, that is to say, *how* children learn is as important as the content of their learning – *what* they learn.

Froebel, Montessori, Pestalozzi, the McMillans and Isaacs left a legacy to early-childhood educators which provides an underpinning of *processes* of learning: the important place of play in young children's learning. There are many interpretations of play, and children's play is something which most adults have witnessed to some extent: in the park, at the shops, at home, in group settings. Play is something which has been experienced by all – humans play. Consequently, everyone might think they know what play is, and perhaps for some such familiarity breeds a form of contempt – in that the importance of play is disregarded simply because it is so much a part of everyone's early (if not later) experiences.

Bruce (1991) examined the views and influences of researchers and theorists including Piaget, Freud, Erickson, Winnicott, Bruner and Vygotsky, and she concluded that there are indeed difficulties in defining play. Yet, play rightly has a prominent place in young children's learning and development. All who watch young children as they play alone and with others know that playing is at the centre stage of learning. But play is not the only means by which children learn; they learn, as Frank Smith might say, 'by the company they keep', by watching and imitating others, by participating in everyday chores and experiences: baking at home, going shopping, going for a walk, helping in the garden, preparing for and participating in family events and celebrations.

Creative and challenging curriculum can incorporate opportunities for play and the realities of daily experiences which overflow with opportunities for teaching and learning. Such realistic learning avenues make for breadth, balance and relevance of learning in early education. Breadth and balance in the curriculum are not just about content but about processes of learning too. Children must be provided with space, time to play, talk, imitate, rehearse, reflect, question and reason as they develop their understanding of things they encounter. Curriculum in early education must value children's processes of making sense and educators must value children's ponderings. Saul (3:9) added some water to dry sand to make it wet. He then began digging in the sand and, with a puzzled look on his face, said, 'There's water in this sand but I can't find it!'

Children must also have opportunities to experience the new and the challenging as 'apprentices' to adults who can help to extend their thinking and doing. Watching craftspeople at work can be a fascinating experience for children who will benefit from opportunities to see people working at their craft: for example, by visiting craft centres where people can be seen making candles, jewellery, knitting, painting, and by inviting people to demonstrate their skills in the nursery such as a carpenter working at the woodwork bench to make a small stool, or a lace-maker, sitting at a low table and working at a piece of lace whilst children watch.

What of the question of curriculum relevance? The Plowden Report was unequivocal: 'At the heart of the educational process lies the child. No advances in policy, no acquisition of new equipment have their desired effect unless they are in harmony with the nature of the child, unless they are fundamentally acceptable to him' (DES, 1967, para. 9). This assertion of the important place of the child at the centre – though seemingly unpopular with policymakers in the 1990s – is a key to the creation of curriculum relevance. Any broadly-based and balanced curriculum if it is to be relevant must have children – as learners – at the centre. Children need opportunities to make sense of their experiences, they need information, opportunities and challenges which incorporate the realities of daily living and stimulate young imaginations.

Children must have opportunities to represent what they see, do and think. They need to represent their ideas and experiences through action, drawing, models, writing and talk. Open-ended materials such as bricks, paint, sand, water and clay enable children to represent their real experiences, their ideas and their imaginings in different ways. Russell used pipes in the water trough to create his representation of a washing machine. He explained, 'This is the washing machine and you put the water in here [funnel] and it's dirty, and you make it go through here [tubing] and you blow and it comes out here, and it's clean!' The co-ordinated schemas of containing and going through a boundary are illustrated in Russell's representation of the washing machine and its effect on the changing state of the water and the clothes.

Children need to work with inventive and creative educators if they are to engage in experimentation, exploration, problem-solving and active thought. To make the most of a meaningful curriculum, children must have space and time as well as materials. They must have time to talk and to be heard. They must have the support and challenge of educators who persistently seek to attune their teaching to children's learning needs and to the structures of children's minds.

Brierley (1987) argued the importance of variety and stimulation. It is through such variety and stimulation that it becomes possible to provide for individuals within a group. Worthwhile experiences, both within the planned learning environment and in the wider community, are rarely narrow or isolated. Experiences and events can develop in numerous ways and where the teaching of the youngest children is based on real experiences and avenues of learning which arise from children's play, there is greater likelihood of achieving curriculum relevance as well as breadth and balance of learning opportunities.

Nourishing young children's forms of thought with worthwhile and interesting content

The curriculum, when planned and presented to children by way of a theme or topic, can help to ensure that a wide range of experiences are linked to provide a variety of experiences which have a curricular balance. If educators think about children's schemas as they plan different themes it is possible to facilitate learning through play and build on children's specific and individual needs and experiences. Consideration of schemas and children's particular 'threads' of thinking can be a way of using theory about how children learn to inform and develop day-to-day practices of teaching. A closer curriculum 'match' can be achieved between the offered curriculum and that which the learner takes up and develops when curriculum content is planned as extensions of what children are already paying attention to, and have demonstrated interest in through their actions, speech and graphic representations.

Children under 5 can assimilate and enjoy a wide range of experiences that extend themes of 'inside', 'surrounding' and 'outside'. Such themes lend themselves to the development of ideas of measurement, mapping, cooking, exploring the environment and making sounds, to name but a few possible avenues for development. Children's schemas, which illuminate their patterns of behaviour and thought, can open the door to a wealth of learning opportunities. Educators who watch children closely are in a position to identify what children are currently paying attention to, and consequently to match curriculum content to children's overriding interests.

Children's schemas seem to sensitise children to certain events and phenomena in their environments. When professionals are able to identify children's interests in this way, they are better placed to select appropriate curricular provision because their work is more clearly informed by knowledge of theory and of children's developments. Children's schemas can be viewed as part of their motivation for learning, their insatiable drive to move, represent, discuss, question, find out. Children are often seen to make clear choices in their play, taking from their environment the elements that interest and attract them and which match their particular and current patterns of interest. For example, a great deal of learning can take place around the simple but fundamental theme of 'what kinds of things can be found or put inside different containers?' This can include trying out simple *en croûte* cookery, food wrapped in pastry, stuffed vine leaves, stuffed peppers, samosas; it can include consideration of animals that live in shells, holes, caves or tunnels.

Effective curriculum should be planned and organised to take account of the need to nourish individual children's schematic concerns, and to provide a wide-ranging curriculum that fosters broad areas of experience and opportunity. Children's and adult's time can be maximised when nurseries are organised as a series of 'workshop' areas, with equipment available for the children to work within specific areas. Learning facilities can include: painting materials; drawing and writing materials; water; sand; woodwork; clay; materials for three-dimensional modellings and construction; imaginative play, miniature figures and models; equipment for fantasy play (hairdressing, dressing up, shop and hospital play); music; books; bricks; home-corner play; and a range of equipment and vehicles for use outdoors. These types of materials form the core of curriculum experiences available for children on a daily basis. Figure 8.1 provides an example of the

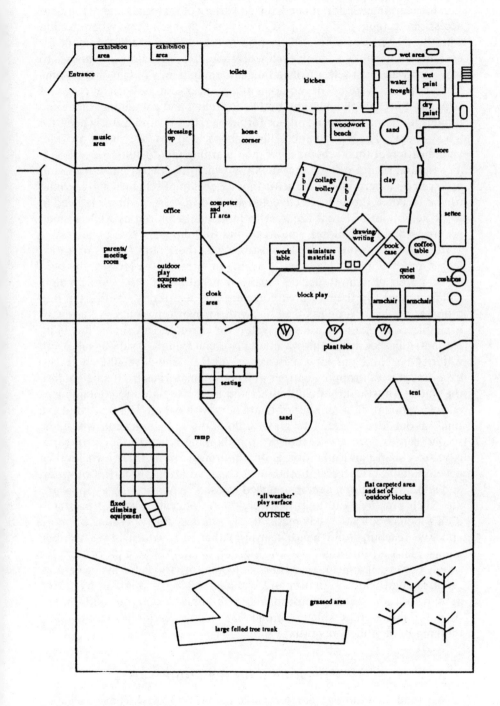

Figure 8.1   Organisation of inside and outside space

organisation of indoor and outdoor space to include the basic daily provision for learning. Children need a wide variety of materials and equipment accessible to them and organised in ways which teach them where to find what they need and where it must be replaced after use. Equipment for each medium can be sited in each workshop area. A child who chooses to play with water can select from a range of equipment what he or she wants to use in the water. The equipment on offer can nourish a range of schemas, for example: jugs and bottles for filling and containing; tubes and funnels for 'going through'; pumps for 'up and down'; and water wheels for 'going round'. The equipment children choose and how they use it provides an indication of their schemas and their learning foci. Adult observation is an essential strand of the curriculum by which the learning needs of children can be ascertained and the further extension of schemas and learning can be facilated through effective and attuned teaching. Educators need to work flexibly in different areas, with individual children as well as small groups to build on children's interests and stimulate new thinking.

Educators of young children must bring to their work 'banks of knowledge' and they might plan their teaching in terms of the tools of the task, but children ultimately decide on the real nature of *their* work. Young children persist in their own explorations and will rarely be diverted into different adult ideas unless they 'fit' with their own pursuits. A variety of available equipment for use with water, for example, can enable flexibility for individual learners whilst a number of children play side-by-side with water. One child pursuing a dynamic vertical schema might choose to experiment with dropping various objects and materials from a height into the water, whilst another child interested in ideas related to containing or enclosing might fill a number of containers with water. The first child can think about ideas related to gravity, flotation and immersion whilst the second can explore events that prompt thinking related to ideas of capacity, size, shape and quantity. Both children work at their own level of development and interest, both have to deal with the properties of water, and adult intervention can be matched to each child's activity as appropriate. Such practices can help early childhood educators to interpret children's behaviour at a schematic level, offering the potential of more effective teaching (and hence learning) than that which arises through adults' plans for introducing a whole group of children to a particular idea simply because it appears on a list of outcomes or targets for the age group. A curriculum which supports and extends children's thinking by taking account of their schemas must include rich human exchanges and a range of material resources which promote and enhance children's learning and thinking to the fullest potential.

Preparation for the future

We need the vision to plan for whole human beings who have a clear and realistic personal identity whatever combination of cultural or religious background, racial origins, gender, ability or disability that may be. Children who know who they are will have the confidence to love and learn and communicate in a world of mathematical, scientific, aesthetic and technological experiences. Children who can collaborate and learn together in harmony with other people are likely to respect and value differences. Children who are able to have intimate responsive relationships with their significant adult will have better access to relevant early learning experiences. Children who play in inspirational, safe and challenging environments will take these values into adulthood and pass them on to future generations. An ethos of respect for and dignity in childhood may be set from the cradle.

(Rouse and Griffin, 1992, pp. 155–6)

Writing above of children aged 0–3 years Rouse and Griffin assert the type of wholeness in learning experiences that children in the 3–5 age range also need and deserve.

There remains much concern about *preparing* children under 5 for the ever-changing National Curriculum which they will encounter from the time they begin statutory schooling. 'Preparation' is a dangerous word when used to refer to young children's education and learning. There can be a tendency to take up the precious years of early childhood and to occupy young children's minds with exercises and training designed to 'get them ready' for the next step, and then the next. Educators can waste time and insult the intellect of young children by requiring them too soon to do things that they will need to do 'when they go to school'. The best way to help children to get ready to be 5-year-olds is to allow them to be 3 when they are 3 and 4 when they are 4. The early experiences which young children thrive on are the best nourishment they can have and the best preparation for the next phase of life they encounter. Being and behaving as a learner and a thinker is the type of preparation for future learning that children need. The experiences and the understanding of young children which have been described in this book underpin much of the knowledge to be acquired through the National Curriculum and offer a richness of curriculum which surpasses the narrowness of pre-school education as defined by *Desirable Outcomes* (DfEE, 1996).

The purpose of education, what it is and how it is carried out, will continue to provide fuel for discussion and writing. John Holt suggests that the education system is driven by three metaphors of which some educators are aware and others are not. Holt argues that these metaphors largely influence what teachers do. This is his description of the first metaphor, which presents education as an assembly line in a bottling or canning factory:

Down the conveyor belts come rows of empty containers of sundry shapes and sizes. Beside the belts is an array of pouring and squirting devices, controlled by employees of the factory. As the containers go by, these workers squirt various amounts of different substances – reading, spelling, maths, history, science – into the containers.

Upstairs, management decides when the containers should be put on the belt, how long they should be left on, what kinds of materials should be poured or squirted into them and at what times, and what should be done about containers whose openings (like pop bottles) seem to be smaller than the others, or seem to have no openings at all.

When I discuss this metaphor with teachers, many laugh and seem to find it absurd. But we need only to read the latest rash of school-improvement proposals to see how dominant this metaphor is. In effect, those official reports all say we must have so many years of English, so many years of math, so many years of foreign language, so many years of science. In other words, we must squirt English into these containers for four years, math for two or three, and so on. The assumption is that whatever is squirted at the container will go into the container and, once in, will stay in.

(Holt, 1991, pp. 148–9)

Pouring in quantities of subject knowledge is not the role of any effective educator. The implication that learners are passive and non-participating beings in the process is both misleading and insulting. Children are active learners who need to learn with and through interaction with knowledgeable educators. For children to learn *with the support of* professional educators rather than *in spite of interferences* from adults, educators must be tuned into young children's thinking, open to their ideas, and responsive to their ever-active minds. The roles of teachers and other early childhood educators who aspire to such quality in learning processes is complex and demanding.

This chapter has suggested ways in which early learning can continue to be progressive, that is: *accelerating, advancing, continuing, continuous, developing, escalating, growing, increasing, intensifying, ongoing*. Real progress in early childhood education depends on the acceptance that children themselves (and their interests) are fundamental to the process of education. A learner- and person-centred early-education curriculum affords children's minds the respect they deserve. Such approaches to curriculum and teaching provide the most effective preparation for the inevitable challenges children will meet and are essential components of philosophy and pedagogy for any curriculum created for thinking children.

9
ASSESSMENT FOR LEARNING

Most teachers waste their time by asking questions which are intended to discover what a pupil does not know, whereas the true art
of questioning has for its purpose to discover what the pupil knows or
is capable of knowing.

(Einstein, 1920)[1]

Assessment for learning is assessment which extends children's learning
because it enhances teaching. All other forms of assessment serve as checks
on whether or not learning has occurred, not as a means – in themselves –
of bringing about learning. The observations in this book include many
examples of teachers observing and interacting with children, making decisions about children's learning and acting upon those decisions to challenge
children further to think, say and do. In that sense, much of this book is
about assessment for learning. But before it is possible to consider more
directly the implications of schemas in the assessment of children's learning, it is necessary to consider the broader picture of assessment in early
education, including the characteristics of assessment for learning, and for
other purposes.

This chapter begins by discussing the place of assessment in early education including, through the example of one child, the place and usefulness
to teaching of Baseline Assessment. The importance to teachers of detailed
observations of children as they learn is highlighted followed by a discussion of some purposes and characteristics of assessment. A consideration of
features of effective early assessment is presented and finally a suggested
method of incorporating observations of children's schemas, decisions
about learning, and next teaching steps is presented.

The place of assessment in early education

Part of any teacher's role is to assess children's learning, their developmental
needs, their need for support, their achievements and their understanding.
Through their work with children, teachers make judgements about children's ideas, what children know, their motivation, their abilities and their
thinking and how their interests and ideas might further be developed. Such
judgements are based more upon what teachers in early education see children do and hear children say rather than formal assessments.

119

Teachers' ongoing assessment begins with careful observation. Observation can help teachers to identify children's achievements and their learning needs and strategies, including their schemas. Worthwhile curriculum content can be matched to children's learning needs once those needs have been identified. Bruce notes the difficulty which teachers might have in observing for a sufficiently long enough period to make meaningful and useful observations; she discusses the dilemma of, as she expresses it, *observing little and often, or more and seldom*:

> The current tendency is towards the former, in spirit; and interestingly, in practice. This is moving away from the traditions of early-years practice, which favoured making lengthy chunks of observations (e.g. Isaacs). It takes some courage to observe less frequently, but for longer and in more depth, especially in the current climate of accountability through the National Curriculum. It takes time to observe. However, the benefit is that depth of observation brings with it a greater breadth of insight into the child's free-flow play, and also into any aspect of learning and development. Teachers in the Freobel Nursery Project (Athey, 1990), and in the Block Play Project (Gura ed, 1992) . . . began to see this with at first shock, and then delight and deep inner satisfaction.
>
> Adults tend to flit from area to area, in an attempt to keep an overview and to give every child attention. This is in an attempt not to neglect any child or area. In reality, this leads to some areas being visited more frequently (e.g. junk modelling), and some children gaining more of the teacher's attention than others. If, on the other hand, we decide to be somewhere for a length of time, we are more likely to take real note of what is happening, simply because we are there long enough to pause and take stock. In fact, this eases the burdensome pressures of observation and recording. It helps us to focus in more depth (and therefore in breadth) on what children know and are learning, rather than constantly worrying about what they don't know, but need to know.
>
> (Bruce, 1991, p. 143)

The either/or choice presented by Bruce might not necessarily be so stark. Observation 'little and often' is quite different in its form and its yield from observation 'more and seldom'. Many of the observations on which this book is based could be described as 'little and often' observations; others, such as 'Sarah' and 'Razia', might be described as 'more and seldom' observations. The point is not so much that teachers need to engage in *either* little and often *or* more and seldom, rather that the sustained practice *over time* of observation of children is necessary and vital to understanding both the short *moments* and more long-term *patterns* of learning.

Assessment which makes use of detailed and focused observations of children should be an ongoing and dynamic process which illuminates children's thinking and their capabilities. To make effective and reliable assessments, teachers need to be open to what children are saying and doing, receptive to their ideas and respectful of their learning agendas. As Moyles puts it:

Children, surprisingly, are themselves frequently the best assessors and testers of what they have learned. Occasionally, they will quite exhaust themselves in proving to themselves and others mastery over a particular activity or material. In assessing children's learning, discussions with the child as an individual can often produce the most useful information, especially as to concepts, knowledge and experiences gained which, when supported with observations and careful records, gives a good overall profile of that child.

(Moyles, 1989, pp. 125–6)

Teachers will always have some things which they want to know about *all* children, but they will find out most about young children as individual and dynamic learners if they develop a way of looking at children with open eyes rather than eyes which are blinkered because only certain aspects of children's abilities are deemed to be of interest or significance in assessment.

Assessment must be located within an effective process of teaching and learning for it is part of a whole and continuous process of educating all young children, and so effective assessment is an essential ingredient of all forms of successful early education.

The following example illustrates some early assessments that take place when a child begins school and will aid discussion of the importance of clarity of purposes for assessment. The child's record begins with score details of his Baseline Assessment, using the QCA scales (QCA, 1997). These scores are followed by an example of a taped conversation, made by his teacher, a few months later.

Figure 9.1 tells us that, according to one particular scale, Robert is a high achiever. However, the score alone tells us nothing about what those achievements are. More information is needed.

BASELINE ASSESSMENT

Name: Robert James

Date of Birth: 6 September 1993

Age at time of assessment: 5y 1m

Total Score | 28

Maximum Score | 32

Figure 9.1

A breakdown, shown in Figure 9.2, of the subscores of each item provides a little information, indicating the areas where Robert achieved maximum points and other areas where he scores less well. Some clue to Robert's strengths is emerging, alongside areas where he might need support to achieve more. But, again, there is insufficient information here for a teacher to decide what to teach next.

Item	Score
Reading A: Reading for meaning and enjoyment	4
Reading B: Letter knowledge	4
Reading C: Phonological awareness	3
Writing	4
Speaking and listening	2
Mathematics A: Number	4
Mathematics B: Using mathematical language	4
Personal and Social Development	3

Figure 9.2

The detail of Robert's achievement on the 32 items on the QCA Baseline Scales (Figure 9.3) shows that Robert failed to score mainly on items involving speaking and listening, and perhaps in interaction with others. Perhaps he is an accomplished early reader? Perhaps he is particularly interested in numbers and what he can do with them? The information available here does not allow a sufficiently detailed picture to be painted. There is insufficient data to act upon – too much 'if', 'perhaps' and 'maybe'.

Robert's teacher needs fuller detail than this scale provides in order to use this assessment fully to inform her teaching. The following transcript of Robert and his teacher working with a calculator illustrates the importance of close observation and interaction in early assessment for learning. Robert aged 5:4 was playing with a calculator. He was pressing in numbers and saying them. This is the conversation which took place between him and his teacher:

Robert: 64
Teacher: Can you think of a number bigger than 64?
Robert: 71
Teacher: 71, is there a number bigger than 71? What's the biggest number you can think of?
Robert: 78
Teacher: Anything bigger?
Robert: 79
Teacher: Anything bigger than 79?
Robert: A hundred!
Teacher: Anything bigger than a hundred?
Robert: *(now with a large grin on his face)* A hundred seventy nine!
Teacher: 179 – anything bigger than that?
Robert: A hundred thousand seventy nine!!
Teacher: That's big – can you get one bigger?
Robert: Let's see *(he uses the calculator and presses the key '7' until the readout window is full of 7s (77777777)* Seven, seven, seven, seven, seven, seven, seven, seven! It can keep going!

	Reading A: Reading for meaning and enjoyment	
1	Holds books appropriately whilst turning the pages and retelling the story from memory	1
2	Able to predict words and phrases	1
3	Uses memory of familiar text to match some spoken and written words	1
4	Reads simple texts	1
	Reading B: Letter knowledge	
1	Recognises his or her own name	1
2	Recognises five letters by shape and sound	1
3	Recognises fifteen letters by shape and sound	1
4	Recognises all letter shapes by names and sound	1
	Reading C: Phonological awareness	
1	Recites familiar rhymes	0
2	Recognises initial sounds	1
3	Associates sounds with patterns in rhyme	1
4	Demonstrates knowledge of sound sequences in words	1
	Writing	
1	Distinguishes between print and pictures in his or her own work	1
2	Writes letter shapes	1
3	Independently writes own name spelt correctly	1
4	Writes words	1
	Speaking and Listening	
1	Recounts events or experiences	1
2	Asks questions to find out information and listens to the answers	1
3	Makes up own story and tells it	0
4	Makes up a story with detail and tells it to a small group, and listens to stories	0
	Mathematics A: Number	
1	Sorts sets of objects by given criterion and explains sorting	1
2	Counts objects accurately	1
3	Shows awareness of using addition	1
4	Solves numerical problems using addition and subtraction	1
	Mathematics B: Using mathematical language	
1	Can describe size	1
2	Can describe position	1
3	Recognises numbers to 10 and writes 1–10	1
4	Can explain an addition sum	1
	Personal and Social	
1	Plays collaboratively	0
2	Is independent and keen to contribute	1
3	Concentrates without supervision for 10 minutes	1
4	Expresses own opinions with a range of adults	1

(QCA Scales 1997)

Figure 9.3

Teacher: That's a big number – is it the biggest you can make?

Robert: Yes! There aren't any more spaces *(on the calculator read out)*

Teacher: But is it the biggest?

Robert: *(pauses for a moment then uses his fingers)* Seven, seven, seven, seven, seven, seven, seven, seven, seven, seven! No! it can be bigger. I can do it ten times on my fingers! They can keep on going and they get bigger.

With his teacher's challenge through questioning Robert arrived at the realisation that numbers can 'keep on going'. This observation shows the use of a calculator, not to work out a calculation but to 'think' about numbers. The size of the number depended at first on the number of spaces (or fingers) Robert had available. At this stage Robert needed that scaffolding for his thinking, but he sufficiently acquired the concept to realise that 'They keep on going.' From this point on, props are unlikely to be necessary in order to make up bigger and bigger numbers.

> To assess attainment it must be observed in the round. Such observation is not easy. The observer has not only to use keenly his eyes and ears, but to know where to direct them: he has not only to see and hear the shape of an event but to perceive its quality.
>
> (Schiller, 1979, p. 3)

Regular and frequent observation is necessary if teachers are to build up a clear picture of individual children, the value of activities and group dynamics. Drummond and Nutbrown (1996) discussed issues related to the observing and assessing of young children. They asked the 'why', 'what', 'how' and 'who' questions of observation and assessment, and suggested that educators will observe and try to understand everything that children do: 'Watching children at their work of interacting with their environment will tell educators some of what they need to know about children's needs and development.'

Throughout this book, observations of children working on their learning have been included to illustrate their capabilities as thinkers and the importance of identifying children's schemas as a way of supporting their learning more precisely. Those who work with young children must see their skills of observation as a means not just to identify end products of learning but to identify children's patterns and pathways of learning as well. Close and systematic observation can identify the threads of children's thinking, their patterns of development and interest. More complete pictures of children's knowing are only obtained when educators are concerned for children as a whole.

Observation such as this needs to be planned for and can be carried out more successfully when the adults who work with young children are prepared to watch with *open eyes* and keep *open minds* about the meaning and importance of what they see (Nutbrown, 1996). Educators must think about what they see and hear children doing and saying. They must create meaning from their observations and be prepared to use what they learn from these processes in their interactions with children. They must trust children to show them what they are learning and they must trust themselves that time spent in observing children though not an easy option is an essential ingredient to effective teaching and learning partnerships.

Purposes of assessment

Different assessment instruments can satisfy different purposes, and decisions about which assessment instruments to use will depend on the purpose of the assessment, and choices about processes and techniques of assessment will depend on the purpose for which the results are to be used.

There are obviously many different reasons for assessment in early education. These can be considered in terms of three broad areas:

- assessment for teaching and learning;
- assessment for management and accountability;
- assessment for research.

Assessment for teaching and learning

Teachers are most interested in the individual diagnoses of learning and development and therefore details of children's knowledge and understanding are of more use than a single summative score (such as Robert's in Figure 9.1) or a list of subscores (Figure 9.2) or even a page of scores allocated to 32 selected items (Figure 9.3). Teachers need the *fine detail* of children's achievement (such as the observation of Robert later working on numbers with his teacher) in order to put together more fitting teaching opportunities, better attuned to the capabilities of the children they teach.

Assessment for management and accountability

This chapter is concerned with assessment for learning (that is, assessment which informs teaching to the point where learning is brought about). But there are others forms of assessment proliferating in the early years which are *not* for teaching purposes (despite often being promoted as such). This alternative to assessment for learning can be described as *assessment for accountability*, and is illustrated by Figures 9.1 to 9.3 where *scores* are given importance over meaning, offering relatively little to the teacher who is concerned with the detail of the individual's achievements. This kind of assessment is carried out to provide a means of holding teachers and schools to account, to provide summary data of the achievements of cohorts according to specified criteria. It is argued that assessments carried out for this purpose have a place, but it cannot be successfully argued that such uses of assessment *in themselves* raise standards or help teachers decide what to teach children next. To the forefront of assessment for accountability is Baseline Assessment of the kind illustrated in the example of Robert earlier in this chapter.

Assessment for research in early education

There are clearly many purposes for *research* in early education and a range of assessment possibilities including those used for teaching and management. Assessment instruments in the *research* category include tools for *evaluation* (of, for example, research programmes, intervention studies, teaching methods and content, national improvement strategies) and instruments which could provide information to help to understand relationships between different factors (e.g. gender and achievement, achievement and poverty, teaching and achievement). One such assessment is the *Sheffield Early Literacy Development Profile* which was developed to measure aspects of early literacy development of 3–5-year-olds (Nutbrown, 1997). This is not to suggest that assessment for research needs to be limited to these kinds of research or these forms of assessment. Clearly, other kinds of research which seek to understand more about early education and children's learning will also use forms of assessment more attuned to assessment for teaching, including talking with children, saving their work, and observing pupils as they play and engage with teachers and other children.

Characteristics of the three purposes of assessment

Early assessment suffers from a problem of terminology. The word 'assessment' is currently in use in several contexts and carries many meanings, both of purpose and practice. Because the same word is applied indiscriminately to all three purposes of assessment discussed here, there is an assumption that a shared understanding exists of what assessment means. This is far from the case. The confusion over terminology can be unravelled if there is clarity of purpose. Figure 9.4 lists the different characteristics of three purposes of assessment: assessment for teaching and learning, assessment for management and accountability, and assessment for research. Of course, these can be subjected to scrutiny and amendment. Nothing is ever quite so neat as to fit, unproblematically, into three columns with an equal number of rows, but the function of this tool is to open up thinking about the *nature* of assessment instruments and processes for each purpose.

Features of effective early assessment

In order to evaluate assessment instruments and assessment processes there are a number of features to consider:

- *Clarity of purpose* Do the instruments state what they are for?
- *Fitness for purpose* Will the instruments be appropriate to the purpose for which they have been designed or selected?
- *Authenticity* Do the tasks in the assessment instrument connect appropriately to how children learn and what children do?

Assessment for Teaching and Learning	Assessment for Management and Accountability	Assessment for Research
focus on individuals	focus on age cohort	focus on samples
concerned with details about each individual learner	concerned with a sample of group performance	concerned with performance of the sample
is ongoing	occurs within specific time frame	takes place at planned points in a study
'takes as long as it takes'	is briefly administered or completed from previous assessment for teaching	can be brief, depends on assessment and ages
needs no numerical outcome to be meaningful	numerical outcome provides meaning	numerical outcome often essential
is open-ended	often consists of closed list of items	often consists of closed items
informs next teaching steps	informs management strategy and policy	informs research decisions, and findings – measures outcomes
information relates primarily to individuals	information relates primarily to classes, schools or areas	information relates to the sample, not to individuals or schools
assessments required for each child	some missing cases permissible	some missing cases permissible
main purpose is teaching	main purpose is accountability	purpose is to add to knowledge
only useful if information is used to guide teaching	only useful when compared to other outcomes (of other measures or cohorts)	only useful as evidence of effectiveness of research study
requires professional insight into children's learning	requires competence in administration of the test	requires competence in administration of the test
depends on established relationship with individuals to be effective	can draw on information derived through interaction with individuals, but not dependent on relationship	often requires no previous relationship, but the ability to establish a rapport with the child at the time of assessment
requires ongoing professional development and experience	requires short training session/learning the test and practice	requires short training session/learning the test and practice

Figure 9.4 Some possible characteristics of three purposes for early assessment

- *Educators who understand the processes of assessment*   Have teachers and other early-childhood educators received appropriate professional development to help them to appraise assessment instruments and conduct assessments appropriately?
- *Processes and outcomes which involve and work for children*   Are children active in assessing their own achievements and efforts? Is children's everyday work taken into account when their learning is assessed?
- *Respect*   Is assessment carried out with proper respect for children's minds? Is adequate time allocated to assessment processes? Are assessment processes scrutinised for their ability to portray achievement? Are the assessments fair and honest, and are all concerned aware of the processes?

Roberts discusses the development of self-esteem in early education settings. She asks a number of questions about assessment:

> Assessment and recording arrangements carry a world of hidden messages for children and parents. Is a positive model used, one which identifies children's special strengths as well as areas for support? Is there accurate and detailed information about children? Do adults make sure that children share their successes, both with their parents and with each other?
> These questions raise some of the issues which have a direct bearing on how children learn to see themselves. Attention to these sorts of details may have a profound effect on children's approach to learning. Our attention to them is surely the entitlement of every child.
> (Roberts, 1995, p. 115)

Assessment is an integral part of teaching. Teachers cannot teach unless they assess. Too often assessment is viewed as an end product of a period of teaching. This might be so where formal national assessments towards the end of statutory schooling lead to examinations and qualifications, but is not the fundamental use of assessment in the early years of education. The most important function of assessment is to help teachers to teach – without *assessment for learning* other forms of assessment are effectively redundant in the drive to improve education and raise achievements, for assessment for learning is a cornerstone of teaching.

Measuring ability in the way many Baseline Assessment schemes suggest will not *in itself* enhance learning. Teachers still need the detail from their own assessments of what children *can* do in order to make decisions about their teaching. Observations and assessments of children's learning, progress, needs, development and interests must be recorded. Formats for written records of children's achievements have proliferated in recent years. Many suggest that learning and progress is recorded in terms of areas of experience, National Curriculum subjects or Desirable Outcomes. This can have the effect of fragmenting our understanding and appreciation of a learning experience or an observation of children playing into several unconnected parts. For example, children playing in a shop may well be involved in sorting and weighing goods (mathematics), they may be

NAME *Danika, Age Four*

OBSERVATION	ANALYSIS OF LEARNING	ACTION	DATE & INITIALS
Following a visit to some flats, D made a construction of cardboard boxes, piling one on top of another using a chair to reach.	Motor and symbolic representation of vertical schema. Work on 'higher' and 'lower'. Introducing vocabulary using appropriate material.	Move into counting boxes. Stabilising structure. More experience of vertical e.g. lifts and escalators.	CN 6.9.91
D. on the climbing frame. Sliding down the slide. She said 'Going down' 'Going up'. Rolling cars and dolls down the slope.	Experimenting with forces and gravity.	More experiences of slopes and rolling experiences. Timing how long it takes to go down.	CN 14.9.91
D. drew a picture. Lots of //// lines. 'This is water falling out of the sky, 'It comes down and goes in the puddles,' D. said.	Understanding early scientific notions of rain and the environment.	Maybe provide different kinds of pouring tools. Showerhead, watering can to encourage observation. Feed in appropriate language.	CN 17.9.91
D's mum reported that D. is going to the top of the stairs and watching a ball bounce to the bottom. She's concerned.	Experiencing gravity and forces again.	Need to provide acceptable safe experiences for observing, bouncing and dropping objects.	CN 25.9.91

Figure 9.5 Danika aged 4

writing lists and cheques (literacy), they may be giving directions of where to deliver a package of groceries (geography) and through it all they are speaking and listening (oracy). In the process of playing and negotiating together they are learning about themselves and their interactions with others (personal and social development).

Play is a vehicle for learning, but play is also the intrinsic part of children's activity. To discard any reference to a play sequence as a whole and to pick out elements which occurred as part of the process is to devalue the holistic in children's activity in favour of the specific segments which adults have decided are important. Assessments and records of children's learning should also include observations of them playing, alone and with others. In so doing, assessment is recorded, as Schiller puts it, 'in the round' and the context and motivation for learning is not lost.

Ways of recording children's learning have been explored by the National Children's Bureau in a set of training materials, Making Assessment Work (Drummond, Rouse and Pugh, 1992). The example in Figure 9.5 has been completed for a 4-year-old who seems to have a predominant interest in a vertical schema.[2]

This format shows one way of making observations and assessments of children's learning and progress. It begins with observations of a child which illuminate the child's needs and interests. The child's key worker notes the observation, her thoughts about the learning which has resulted and, importantly, what is to happen next, that is, the action the educator will take. Dates of the observation and initials of the worker are useful for checking and reflecting at a later date. Parents can also contribute to such records. Some parents are happy to offer observations and discuss the resulting learning and consequent actions with teachers who spend time in such dialogues. Records such as these can become part of a child's achievement profile. Clear details of what children can do need to be developed in a form which children's future teachers can use and build on effectively as children's learning develops. Using schemas as a focus for some of these observations ensures that children's actions as well as their learning are recorded. This means that 'what happened' can be noted, learning identified and further curriculum opportunities and experiences can be planned to match children's actions and understandings.

This book is about assessment in that it provides examples of *assessment for learning*, which – like no other – extends children's learning, for such assessments are used by teachers to inform and enhance teaching.

Notes

1. I thank my colleague Peter Hannon for finding Einstein's words for me.

2. This format was first published in *Making Assessment Work* (Drummond, Rouse and Pugh, 1992) and is reproduced here with permission.

10
WORKING WITH PARENTS

Five-year-old Sarah was playing in the garden of her house. It was a bright sunny day and she was bathing her doll. She skilfully carried jugs of warm water from the kitchen and poured them into the baby bath, taking care not to overfill the jug and checking after each jugful to see if there was enough water in the bath. She checked the temperature of the water with her arm and told her friend, 'You do that to check that they don't scald their skin, babies' skin is so soft, if the temperature is too hot they could burn.' Sarah undressed her doll and went into the kitchen to put the clothes in the sink. 'I'll wash them later when the baby is asleep. They don't go in the machine, it makes the knitting go a funny shape,' she explained. Returning to the garden she carefully put the doll into the bath, gently splashing the water over its body. She soaped its head, taking care not to get soap in its eyes. 'It stings if soap gets in and then he'll cry.' Sarah babbled and cooed to the baby doll in a sing-song sort of voice and then spoke to it. 'We'll decide what you want to wear today when you're dry.' Lifting the baby doll out of the water she laid it gently on a towel set out ready. She wrapped the towel around the doll and cradled it in her arms while she sang part of a lullaby. Then, holding the doll in one arm and resting on her hip, she began sorting through a basket of doll's clothes with the other hand. 'The green one today I think. It's sunny but it is a bit windy and this is nice and woolly and thick and warm.' She dressed the doll, chatting about the weather, about going to the shops in the pram and added, 'and then when you're asleep Mummy will wash your clothes and have a cup of coffee and watch *Playdays*'.

What did Sarah know? What can be learned from watching a child playing in this way? She knew about capacity, degrees of fullness and emptiness. She knew about temperature, the terminology related to this and the consequences of water being too hot in the baby bath. She knew about the need to keep warm by wearing woollen clothing. She knew that bathing a baby took time, that it was important, and could be a loving and pleasurable exchange, a special time which involves talking, touching and cuddling. She knew that caring and loving were experiences to give time to and to enjoy. This display of competent and human interaction is an example of a whole and worthwhile learning experience. From whom did she learn these things? How did she know what to do? In this scenario, a little girl was using her knowledge acquired through helping her mother to care for her new baby brother. Her actions, her language and her disposition reflected the loving and sensitive encounters and routines she had witnessed between her mother and the baby.

Recognising parents' roles as educators

Attitudes of partnership
Educators must show a recognition of parents' roles in children's learning if children's learning and development opportunities are to be maximised. Professional educators will inevitably hold different attitudes towards parents depending on their ideologies and experiences. A multidisciplinary group discussed their perception of the role of parents making the following comments that illustrate some of the ways in which professional educators think about parents as their children's primary educators.

> Many parents can help with planning in an informal sense. Not necessarily at a planning meeting but in terms of helping staff identifying their children's needs and their expectations as parents and trying to find ways of satisfying them.
>
> (Nursery teacher)

> Professionals forget that parents know their children first.
>
> (Day nursery officer)

People who work with young children can positively enhance opportunities they offer children through work with parents. Parents and professional educators both have important and distinctive roles, so an attitude is needed where these roles are recognised and respected (to the benefit of the children). As Athey puts it:

> Parents and professionals can help children separately or they can work together to the great benefit of the children. Parents can give practical help in classrooms (as many already do), but perhaps the greatest benefit to teachers in working with parents is the spur towards making their own pedagogy more conscious and explicit.
>
> (Athey, 1990, p. 66)

An attitude towards parents whereby teachers and other educators are prepared to think about and articulate their own pedagogy and to discuss it with parents and the wider community is now essential in the development of effective early education.

Collaborative relationships
Early childhood educators must continue to examine their own feelings about working with parents. The idea of partnership with parents is for some an integral and essential part of their work, whilst for others it is a threatening prospect. All who work with young children must take time to examine for themselves their own deeply held beliefs about professional involvement with parents of the children with whom they work. Sharing

pedagogy with parents can be like opening doors to a new world. Parents will have watched their children fill and empty cupboards, do 'twizzies' in the garden, walk along the tops of walls, and try not to step on the gaps between paving stones as they walk along the pavements. Putting inter-pretations of understanding on to these commonly observed traits of child-hood gives insight into children's learning about space and position, movement and height.

Some professional educators feel that they want to share their under-standing and professional knowledge with parents about how children learn, and they want parents to feel that their contribution will be positively welcomed. Collaborative relationships between parents and pro-fessional educators that incorporate a sharing of pedagogy can enhance children's learning. Reporting on the Froebel Early Childhood Project, Athey noted the importance of participation:

> One of the most important outcomes of the project was that all the adults watched and listened with ever-increasing interest to what the children were saying and doing. Nothing gets under a parent's skin more quickly and more permanently than the illumination of his or her own child's behaviour. The effect of participation can be profound.
>
> (Athey, 1990, p. 66)

The development of effective relationships between parents and nurseries, schools, playgroups and crèches needs effort and commitment. A survey of parents and teachers in Maryland, USA (Junior Achievement, 1991) stated that barriers to co-operation existed within parent and teacher groups and that parents and teachers blamed each other for the lack of parental involvement.

Parents' views of themselves as their children's educators

Parents of the children described in this book were asked what part they felt they played in helping their children to learn. There were three main types of reaction:

- Parents who did not recognise the things they did as helping their children to learn.
- Parents who felt that they helped 'informally' at home.
- Parents who felt they did a lot to help their children to learn but felt that the benefits of nursery education enhanced what they could do.

Parents who did not recognise the things they did as helping their children to learn commented:

> He plays at nursery. He doesn't play at home. He's too naughty, he doesn't learn anything from me. But he learns at nursery so that's OK.

> I don't think it is for me to help him learn at home, I think that's what nurseries are for. If he wants to play with his toys he can but I don't

believe that home should be all about education too. They have to learn in nursery and when they go to school.

I make sure she's got toys and things to keep her amused, but I don't think it's up to me to start trying to get her to learn colours and numbers and things like some people do.

Parents who felt that they helped 'informally' at home commented:

I do things like singing nursery rhymes when she goes to bed.

I don't 'teach' her as such but I do talk to her about the things she's interested in and answer her questions.

I let him help me to make tea, he loves mixing things for cakes, and he helps with doing the washing and tidying up.

We haven't got a garden and the twins love to climb so I take them to the play area at the bottom of the road most days. They run and climb and play hide-and-seek. They love it.

Parents who felt they did a lot to help their children to learn but that the benefits of nursery education enhanced what they could do commented:

There are more things to do here than at home. I have jigsaws and drawing and things, but here they've got water and sand and those kinds of things to learn about too.

I read to her at home and we look at the pictures more, I do more with books now, picking up ideas from you.

I like going on outings with the nursery. Then when we get home we can talk about it and look at the things she collected. Then usually we bring them for you to look at with her again the next day to put on the table for the others to see too.

Parents who are informed about ways in which children learn and think, and how they represent their thoughts through talk, drawing and action are in a better position to support the continuity and progression of their children's learning and development between home and nursery, school or other group setting. Parents who understand what their children do, and see that it has some value to their learning and cognitive development, will be in a better position to discuss these things with teachers and other educators. Some parents are well informed and ensure that they obtain the information they need. However, it is the responsibility of professional educators to make sure that all parents have access to, and opportunities to discuss, information that is relevant to their children. Those responsible for educational provision for young children should recognise the need to allocate time and resources to work with parents. If equality of opportunity is to mean anything in practice, parents of all children should have opportunities to read, discuss and reflect with their children's educators upon current research. If this happens, parents may be less inclined to value the 'perfect' painting above the dynamic representation of something the child has seen, but which needs interpretation and is perhaps less aesthetically pleasing. Research suggests that many parents value this kind of involvement and information (Smith, 1980; Bennett, 1990; Weinberger, 1996). With this in mind the next section discusses the need to exchange information with parents and ways in which this can take place.

Exchanging information with parents

The Froebel Early-Education Project (Athey, 1990) was important for a number of reasons. Perhaps most significant were involvement of parents, involvement of professional educators and the identification of effective ways of discussing children's patterns of learning with parents (sharing pedagogy). This linking of three important elements, parents, professionals and pedagogy, is discussed by Athey (*ibid.*, p. 207): 'The professionals identified schemas but, once identified, parents were able to give examples . . . Professionals have useful knowledge but it is not always shared with parents'.

Another important finding of the Froebel project highlighted the importance of early experiences. This included visits to buildings, parks, gardens, events and watching people dancing, riding, demonstrating their skills and crafts. Parents and children often shared these experiences and Athey reports that, as the project progressed, parents talked more with their children, pointed things out and attended with interest to what was happening and what their children were paying attention to.

Perhaps the most important elements of the Froebel project were strategies developed to identify and nourish children's schemas, and to involve parents and professionals in pedagogical dialogue which resulted in children having their parents actively involved in their learning. If Athey's work is to be of value to professional educators and the children with whom they work, ways need to be found further to incorporate Athey's 'three *P*s': *Parents, Professionals* and *Pedagogy*, into practice.

Group meetings

Many nurseries and schools hold meetings for parents to explain what happens in the establishment, the philosophy and ethos of the school, to introduce parents to facilities available such as the toy library, book library, and so on. Some nursery schools have held successful 'workshop' evenings for parents where activities are set out for parents to try and where staff can explain the educational purposes behind the provision they make for the children. Early-childhood educators are now working hard to share their knowledge with parents, to explain why they do what they do. Such meetings for parents have a valuable place in developing a partnership and enhancing understanding.

There have been some exciting developments in the area of sharing ideas about schemas with parents. Usually discussion about schemas begins with a teacher or nursery nurse mentioning something to one parent and then the interest grows. In my experience of working with parents I have been privileged to work with staff responsible for nursery schools and classes and reception classes, and to talk with small groups of parents about children's schemas and their children's patterns of development.

Group meetings can begin by viewing slides of children doing familiar activities: using the climbing frame, hiding in a tent, operating the water wheel, filling containers with sand, filling the washing machine, lining up vehicles in a 'traffic jam'. Parents, of course, immediately recognise these things as familiar, and sometimes talk about other similar activities which children do at home: hiding under the bed clothes, making dens behind the sofa, investigating locks and keys, fascination with holes. From this kind of discussion, the familiar and immediately recognisable, the idea of pattern and of schemas can be introduced. Commonly, parents reflect on the patterning behaviour of their own children and make comments similar to those made by this group of parents:

So that's why she likes to wrap the knives and forks up in a serviette!

Now I realise that he's not doing it to spite me but he just needs to collect things in little bags!

Perhaps that's the reason that his pockets are always filled with stones!

I thought she was being naughty when she kept tying legs of chairs together, now I think perhaps she's doing a 'connecting' schema!

These remarks are typical of the things parents say once they have an insight into their children's patterns of thinking. At one meeting for parents children's fascination with filling sinks with water was discussed. Some parents found it helpful to think of such behaviour from the point of view of the children asking themselves, 'What will this water do? What will happen if . . .?' Seeing the child's fascination with the water rather than seeing the flooded bathroom as an evil wrongdoing helped them understand things from the child's viewpoint. Discouraging such behaviour by understanding and providing a different way to explore water is more satisfying for parent and child and a positive experience where something is learned rather than something which attracts guilt and punishment.

One mother, after the discussion told the nursery teacher the next day:

I never thought of playing in the sink with water as anything to do with learning. I went home after the meeting. Together we filled the paddling pool. I showed her how the water went from the tap down the pipe. We filled it really full and she got in and some water overflowed. It was terrific. She laughed and played for ages. Pouring water from one container to another, she splashed some out onto the grass. I used to say, 'Don't let it out – if you do I'm not putting any more in.' Yesterday I topped it up because it was all learning for her. I hope we have more meetings. It helps me to see how she's learning from ordinary everyday things, and I can see it now.

(Mother of child aged 3:7)

Some parents described their experiences of group meetings:

I like it when we talk in a group about our children, what they can learn and how they play, and how that helps to learn. I can see how the toys and painting and playing teach them.

I really understand now what they get out of playing in nursery. I can see that it's not just nice for them to come and be with other children. It's teaching them. The teachers really know ways of getting them to learn – while they're playing.

The meetings help me to learn about helping him at home – like talking to him about what he's doing.

It's nice to be able to say 'My Kim does so and so' and the teacher can explain what she's learning and what I can do at home to help.

We talked about Maths one week. I never thought about all those boxes and yoghurt pots and tubes I save as teaching them about shape. Now we talk about shapes of boxes and things when we're unpacking shopping sometimes and we count things too. I thought she was too young for Maths, but they do a lot in nursery, but not forced – more by playing.

I think all parents should have meetings to find out about children learning early on.

We did writing. I thought – when I got the letter about the meeting – that it was stupid. But I can see how they do begin playing and pretending to write like letters and shopping lists really young. Sadie does and I encourage her now.

When you've been to a few meetings you feel like you've done a real good job teaching them things from when they were little. It's very good because you see your children in a different way.

Educators need to move on from identifying patterns of behaviour to explaining to parents how they use such knowledge of schemas to plan and provide for learning. The value of experience can also be discussed with parents, presenting the idea of giving children different shared experiences. Children whose parents take them to different and interesting places at weekends are better placed to extend their ideas than children who only ever spend their time in the house or in the back garden. But all parents should have the opportunity to know about ways to support their children's ideas and extend their experiences. Parents who cannot afford expensive outings can still involve their children in a range of experiences by using the local shop, the nearby playground, local allotments, a garage, talking about roadworks or happenings at a nearby building site. Schools, nurseries and other educational provision should incorporate such experiences into their curriculum and involve parents in such planned happenings.

Notices, leaflets, booklets

As well as planned times for shared dialogue to talk with parents it is also helpful to have some written information. Notices as part of an exhibition of children's work can, alongside children's drawings and photographs of them in action, give parents and other visitors insights into the value of what is happening. This is most useful when the drawings do not resemble

what children say about them and when parents sometimes see an apparent
'chaos' of children playing and working when they arrive to take children
home. Information presented in this way can help to communicate the idea
that though learning looks (and is) messy, there is valuable and important
work going on.

The following examples illustrate ways in which the main points of an
exhibition of children's work can be explained. The first notice appeared in
the centre of a pinboard which displayed photographs of children mixing
paint and painting on large sheets of paper. Some photographs showed two
children building up 'patchwork' paintings in a wonderful array of colours.
These paintings were finally covered in a layer of thick brown paint that
obliterated all trace of pattern and colour. One child then folded her painting into a small square. The two paintings, one folded, were displayed with
the photographs and the notice to parents read:

> These children have been interested in shapes that they can fit to-
> gether. They fitted together patches of colour and then covered them
> with one colour. They are 'enclosing' space, and shape, and putting
> different things inside things. They are learning about space, size,
> colour and pattern. We thought you would like to see the photo-
> graphs as well as the final products to see the work that went into it!

Another example of this kind of information-sharing was on an exhibition
of children's drawings and paintings. The work consisted of children's representations of vertical actions and objects. There was a drawing of a
ladder against a wall and the child's comment, 'I helped to fix the broken
window'. Another painting showed an aeroplane and something dropping
out of the bottom. The child had explained, 'We went to the air show. The
lady jumped out and landed on the field, she was OK but there was an
ambulance there in case.' The notice on this display read:

> Some of the children are interested in things which go up and down.
> They have painted pictures and made drawings which show 'up and
> down' things. They have learned a lot from watching things they have
> seen and can draw them and talk about them. Some people call the
> work children do about 'up and down' part of a Vertical Schema. This
> means that children's ideas seem to fit with a pattern of things that
> move vertically. Nursery staff will tell you more if you are interested.

Several parents found this interesting and asked for more information. They
also had other examples of vertical schema to share: 'Paul keeps dropping
things out of his bedroom window. I go crazy when he does it, but perhaps
it's his schema. I'm not going to let him do it but I'm glad he's not just being
naughty.' This parent made an important point. It is one thing to understand
and recognise children's schemas and tune in to their patterns of development, but it does not mean that children must be allowed to do things which
are dangerous, socially unacceptable or, perhaps, just inconvenient at the
time. The teacher and parents talked about ways to encourage Paul's fascination with dropping things from a height which satisfied him and that were not
a danger to himself, household contents or passers-by!

One parent remarked on the importance of taking children to see different things:

> I usually take her out to keep her occupied and because it's nice to go out together. I don't know why, because it's so obvious, but I never thought of it actually giving her things to think about and things to learn about. I'll notice what she does more now when we go to different places.

It is useful to have literature available in the form of brief leaflets or short booklets for parents who want to read about schemas and children's patterns of learning.

Talking with individual parents

As well as sharing information in group meetings and in a written form, time when parents and their children's professional educators can talk together is essential. This is often easier said than done in the busy atmosphere of classroom or other group setting. Those responsible for staffing funding or provision must be continually reminded that working effectively with young children means working effectively with their parents and that this takes time. There is no substitute for talking about children with parents on an individual basis. This needs to be an ongoing practice, where parents can share what has happened at home, educators can share occurrences in the group and together understandings and interpretations can be made.

Athey's project involved time in talking with parents on an individual basis. Often the activities described earlier, meetings, notices and booklets can be supported by individual, more personal conversations.

Assessment

More and more parents are becoming involved in recording children's development, and there is much to say about early assessment as a whole. Examples of children's play and learning at home can add to records of children's learning and development and contribute to assessment procedures.

Principles of partnership

As centralisation of control over the education of young children increases, the establishment of principles upon which the education of young children is based becomes more important. It is necessary for educators to decide where they stand, and why they do what they do and believe what they believe about young children's learning. Other writers have discussed their principles of early childhood education (Brierley, 1987; Bruce, 1987). There has also been discussion of the principles that should underpin the assessment of children's learning and development (Drummond, Rouse and Pugh, 1992; Drummond and Nutbrown, 1996) and quality of provision (Nutbrown, 1998).

If professional educators are to move forward their work in partnership with parents, they must decide the principles upon which these partnerships are based. This chapter concludes with six principles of partnership which educators can consider as they decide what partnership with parents means for them and their own principles which underpin the work they do with young children and their families. These six principles are:

- parents are the primary carers and educators of their children;
- consistency, continuity and progression;
- equality of opportunity;
- working in the interests of children;
- respect;
- the 'loving use of power'.

Clarity of meaning is important in the establishment of principles. Each principle needs to be carefully and clearly articulated so that everyone is clear about the meaning and implications of the principles they share.

Principle 1: Parents are the primary carers and educators of their children
Everyone who works with young children, whether in schools or other settings, should acknowledge the primary role of parents as carers and educators of their children. Parents have clear responsibilities for their children's living and learning experiences. There needs to be two-way dialogue, consultation, information and partnership. Parents are the first and primary educators of their children, and they entrust their children's minds to nurseries, playgroups and schools for small but crucial moments of their lives. Between the ages of 5 and 16, children attend school for about 15,000 hours, that is about 625 days, less than two years.

Principle 2: Consistency, continuity and progression
There must be consistency in the kinds of involvement which educators have with parents. Do parents know to whom they can talk? Are there key people who will always make themselves available to parents? Do some staff members have responsibility for developing work (and partnership) with parents? Is there consistency of expectations between the school, nursery or group and parents? Is there a consistent and understood philosophy of partnership with parents?

If initiatives to involve parents are set up, there needs to be consideration of how such developments might be sustained. What kinds of continuity of involvement might there be? What is it realistic to do? How might successful projects keep going over time? What might be done to ensure some kind of progression and development of parental involvement and partnerships between the home and the group? Does involvement and partnership always remain at the level of a valuable Tuesday morning classroom-reading workshop? Does it remain at the level of fundraising for the group? Does it remain at the level of the weekly rota shift at the playgroup? Or does partnership develop from these kinds of things into a climate where parents work with professional educators in many different ways, co-operating, debating, sharing concerns and excitements together in a two-way process?

Principle 3: Equality of opportunity
Is the important role of *all* parents acknowledged? Do *all* parents believe that the workers who spend time with their children want them as parents to be involved? What of black parents, single parents, parents living in extreme poverty, parents with disabilities, parents who often complain and ask difficult questions, parents of children with special educational needs, are they *all* involved in the life of and developments within the group setting as far as they wish to be? Or do educators in group settings select in some way the parents who they feel will be the 'best' fitted for the roles they have defined for them?

Principle 4: Working in the interests of children
Are partnerships with parents developing in the interests of children? Is their learning and development, their self-esteen and their thinking being enhanced because there is a spirit of co-operation between education professionals and parents? Are the children always of mutual concern? Sometimes this may mean that staff and parents need to talk about things which give rise to feelings of anger, vulnerability and discomfort. Discussions may result in parents and staff feeling challenged or vulnerable. Sometimes parents and their children's teachers must discuss events, incidents and practices concerning which they might wish they could leave well alone; and there may be difficult things to say and hear. Parents need to be able to ask why certain practices are adopted and workers must be able to articulate their reasons for doing things. Working in the interests of children means parents and professionals maintaining dialogue around a range of issues, both welcome and unwelcome.

Principle 5: Respect
Crucially, do workers and parents have a respect for each other? Do they understand and respect their respective roles and skills? Do they value the parts they both play in the lives of young children? Educators in group settings, teachers, nursery nurses, playgroup workers and crèche workers must respect themselves. They must respect the parents of the children they work with, respecting them in their vital role as an essential and unique person in the lives of their children. Respect for each other is a necessary part of a fertile and lasting partnership. Respect is bound up in each person's feelings about the work they do and the people they meet as a part of their work. But we need to be clear what we mean by respect:

> Respect is not about 'being nice' – it is about being clear, honest, courteous, diligent and consistent.

> (Nutbrown, 1998, p. 36)

Principle 6: The 'loving use of power'
Educators and parents are very powerful people in the lives of young children. Drummond (1993) discussed teachers' strong feelings about the idea of themselves as 'powerful' people. She noted that the teachers she worked with saw 'power' as overwhelmingly negative and argued that this denial of their own power was disconcerting. Drummond *(ibid.,* p. 173) wrote: 'We do have the power to educate, for a better world, the children in our schools; to deny this power is, by extension, to deny our real responsibilities to children.'

It is important that the powerful people in children's lives, parents and professional educators, admit their power and make 'loving use' of it (Smail, 1984). It is their responsibility, though they may often feel 'powerless', to acknowledge that in the eyes of young children they are sometimes 'all powerful'. They can crush some children with a frown or make them feel on top of the world with a smile. The 'loving use of power' is an essential principle of partnership.

If the six principles of partnership discussed here are to be enacted, and if parents' wishes for the best of education for their youngest children are to be achieved, there is a need for educators who are appropriately trained and qualified and whose qualifications have the same credibility and rigour as those who work with older children. In 1993 the then Secretary of State for Education proposed changes to the training of teachers who work with young children that included lower entry qualifications and shorter courses. The implication here was that working with young children was a less complex job and therefore less training was needed. This proposal was withdrawn after it prompted protests from parents, teacher training establishments and teachers though changes to the initial training of teachers continue. Ironically such a proposal came at a time when there was also the beginnings of discussion about degree qualifications for those working with children under 3 years old.

Some parents were discussing the importance of highly trained and qualified staff. One parent remarked to her daughter's nursery teacher, 'You've got her mind to see to. I need to know that you know what you're doing. I wouldn't let just anyone operate on her brain unless I knew they knew what they were doing. I don't want just anyone with a little bit of information teaching her either.'

Work with parents needs to be based on firmly established principles of partnership. If parents and professional educators treat each other with mutual respect, if they acknowledge that they each have different, separate and important skills, if they share the things that are important about children's learning, they can support children's learning and extend their thinking in a fundamental way. Athey's work has demonstrated effective learning where parents and professionals talk together and observe the children, and where professionals are prepared to articulate their thinking and share their expertise.

It has been argued previously (Nutbrown, Hannon and Weinberger, 1991) that teachers need training opportunities to develop their work with parents in order to promote children's early literacy development. The REAL (Raising Early Achievement in Literacy) Project has developed ways of working with parents to enhance four particular roles in children's learning: providing *opportunities*; showing *recognition*; *interaction* with children; and being a *model* (Nutbrown and Hannon, 1997). A framework which teachers can use to work with parents to enhance these four roles in literacy has also been developed and evaluated (Hannon and Nutbrown, 1977). Very few opportunities exist either in the initial training of teachers or through later professional development for teachers to develop their skills, confidence and thinking in the area of work with parents. Much of the work on parental involvement which once took place in the initial training of teachers has effectively been eroded to make more time to fulfil legislative requirements in teacher education. Whilst the Education Reform Act 1988 was aimed at placing parents in the 'driving seat' of education, what has happened is that parents have become excluded from the curriculum as they have instead been recruited on governing bodies, and fundraising or finance committees. The result is a growing number of teachers who lack confidence in working closely with parents.

This lack of professional development opportunities with regard to work with parents was highlighted in the early stages of work to implement Baseline Assessment of children beginning school. In January 1996 the then Secretary of State for Education and Employment asked SCAA to survey current practice on baseline assessment and to draft proposals for consultation. SCAA discussion papers for conferences on Baseline Assessment included the following statement about parents:

> The Secretary of State in her letter giving the remit to carry out an initial survey and consultation on baseline assessment stressed the vital role that parents play in the education of such young children and asked SCAA to make the consultation of parents a high priority. The existing baseline assessments vary widely in the amount of parental involvement. The input of parents into any form of baseline assessment is felt to be very important by many authorities who feel that parents are able to make a worthwhile contribution to the processes as they know the achievements and interests of their child. Other authorities hold parents evenings to give feedback to the parents about the assessment rather than using the parent as a source of information.
>
> (SCAA, 1996, paper 4)

Participants in consultation conferences were asked if they thought that parents should be asked to give an input into Baseline Assessment and what part they could play, and further consultation reiterated the importance of *'looking at the role of parents'* (SCAA, 1996). However, it was concluded that:

> There was widespread agreement with the principle of involving parents/carers at an early stage. There was a general reluctance,

however, from those working in schools about additional requirements. Many made the point that many teachers have had little training in talking with parents/carers and do not find it easy to pass on
accurate judgements about children's achievements, particularly if
children are achieving below the average for the class.

(SCAA, 1997, para 13)

Despite SCAAs alarming finding that teachers felt ill-equipped to talk to
parents about their children's achievements, its recommendations failed
adequately to address this issue. Instead it was recommended that teachers
attend one day of training which would focus on:

> administration of baseline assessment, the use of its outcomes and
> reporting to parents/carers.

(*Ibid.*, para 33)

There is no recommendation that teachers receive fuller professional development to enable them to focus on assessment issues, research and
research implications, and purposes of assessment or indeed on the role of
parents in assessment.

Early-childhood educators need to develop their skills in the area of
sharing pedagogy with parents and they need access to professional development in order to fulfil this aspect of their role.

ENDWORD

Children need teachers who engage in professional and sensitive reflection, who think about their work and who respond to new ideas and new experiences drawn from reflection on their practice and relevant research. Children need early-childhood educators who are supported in attending fora where professional dialogue about pedagogy and children's learning takes place. Children need teachers who see the development of their own knowledge and responsiveness as a part of their responsibility as a teacher.

Threads of Thinking has presented and discussed aspects of children's learning, interwoven with consideration of the complex role of teaching young children. If children's minds are to be nourished and their amazing ability to think and learn is to be acknowledged and respected, educators working with young children, in whatever setting, must realise these different and demanding roles.

Children's minds are valuable and precious. Young children must receive the respect and recognition they deserve as capable thinkers and learners. Part of this respect should be demonstrated by ensuring that the adults who work with young children are appropriately trained, properly qualified, fittingly experienced to manage the diversity of the task, and respected as members of a professional group who receive due reward and recognition for their work. Many children under 5 attend other settings which are staffed with educators who do not have graduate status or the benefit of extended professional training or development. Children in these settings are equally entitled to a high level of quality experience, they are equally entitled to work with adults who are able to recognise and fulfil the important roles and responsibilities of educators. To aspire to this kind of quality in a diversity of provision for children there must be initial training and inservice professional development opportunities for all workers to explore and discuss in depth the competencies and potential of *all* young children. There must be more networking of provision for people working with young children in different settings to meet together and discuss their observations of children's learning.

If policy, practice and pedagogy become sufficiently attuned to the learning needs of *all* young children the early twenty-first century can be the time when the right of *all* young children to learn in the company of well-educated educators is realised.

REFERENCES

Abbot, L. and Moylett, H. (eds) (1997) *Working with the Under 3s: Responding to Children's Needs*, Open University Press, Buckingham.

Ahlberg, J. and Ahlberg, A. (1982) *Funny Bones*, Picture Lions, London.

Ahlberg, J. and Ahlberg, A. (1986) *The Jolly Postman or Other People's Letters*, Heinemann, London.

Alborough, J. (1986) *Willoughby Wallaby*, Walker Books, London.

Alborough, J. (1989) *Cupboard Bear*, Walker Books, London.

Allan, P. (1989) *Who Sank the Boat?*, Picture Puffin, Harmondsworth.

Anderson, H. C. (1992) 'The Emperor's New Clothes', in Ash, N. and Higton, B. (eds) *Fairy Tales from Hans Anderson – A Classic Illustrated Edition*, Pavilion Books, London.

Armstrong, M. (1990) 'Another way of looking', *Forum*, Vol. 33, No. 1, pp. 12–16.

Arnold, C. (1990) 'Children who play together have similar schemas'. Unpublished project report submitted as part of the Certificate in Post-Qualifying Studies validated by the National Nursery Examining Board.

Athey, C. (1981) 'Parental involvement in nursery education', *Early Child Development and Care*, Vol. 7, No. 4, pp. 353–67.

Athey, C. (1986) Unpublished course material for INSET, Sheffield LEA, 26–28 February.

Athey, C. (1990) *Extending Thought in Young Children: A Parent–Teacher Partnership*, Paul Chapman Publishing, London.

Bahti, M. (1988) *Pueblo Stones and Storytellers*, Treasure Chest Publications, Tucson, Arizona.

Barnsley LEA (1990) *Developing Literacy Through Structured Play*, Barnsley LEA, Barnsley.

Bayley, N. and Mayne, W. (1981) *The Patchwork Cat*, Jonathan Cape, London.

Beck, I. (1989) *The Teddy Bear Robber*, Doubleday, Toronto.

Bennett, D. (1990) 'Happily to School', *Topic*, Issue 3, Spring 1990.

Bennett, J. (1991) *Learning to Read with Picture Books*, The Thimble Press, London.

Bissex, G. L. (1980) *GYNS AT WRK – a Child Learns to Write and Read*, Harvard University Press, Cambridge, Mass.

Brierley, J. (1987) *Give Me a Child until He is Seven: Brain Studies and Early Childhood Education*, Falmer Press, London.

Briggs, R. (1980) *The Snowman*, Puffin, Harmondsworth.

Brown, R. (1973) *A First Language*, Allen & Unwin, London.

Brown, R. (1983) *A Dark, Dark Tale*, Scholastic Publications, London.

Bruce, T. (1987) *Early Childhood Education*, Hodder & Stoughton, London.

Bruce, T. (1991) *Time to Play in Early Childhood Education*, Hodder & Stoughton, London.

Bruce, T. (1992) 'Children, adults and blockplay', in Gura, P. (ed.) *Exploring Learning – Young Children and Blockplay*, Paul Chapman Publishing, London.

Bruner, J. (1960) *The Process of Education*, Harvard University Press, London.

Bruner, J. (1977) *The Process of Education*, Harvard University Press, Cambridge, Mass.

Burningham, J. (1963) *Borka – the Adventures of a Goose with No Feathers*, Jonathan Cape, London.

Burningham, J. (1978) *Mr Gumpy's Outing,* Puffin, Harmondsworth.

Burningham, J. (1980) *The Shopping Basket*, Jonathan Cape, London.

Burningham, J. (1991) *Oi! Get Off Our Train*, Red Fox, London.

Butterworth, N. (1991) *One Snowy Night*, Picture Lions, London.

Butterworth, N. (1995) *Jasper's Beanstalk*, Picture Lions, London.

Campbell, R. (1984) *Dear Zoo*, Puffin, Harmondsworth.

Campbell, R. (1988) *My Presents*, Campbell Blackie Books, London.

Carr, W. (1995) *For Education*, Open University Press, London.

Carroll, L. (1865) *Alice's Adventures in in Wonderland*.

Carroll, L. (1871) *Through the Looking Glass and What Alice Found There*.

Cartwright, R. and Kinmouth, P. (1979) *Mr Potter's Pigeon*, Hutchinson Junior Books, London.

Catley, A. (1989) *Jack's Basket*, Beaver Books, London.

Chapman, A. J. and Foot, H. C. (eds) (1976) It*'s a Funny Thing Humour*, Pergamon Press, Oxford.

Chauduri, A. (1998) *A Strange and Sublime Address*, Vantage, London.

Christie, J. F. (ed.) (1991) *Play and Early Literacy Development*, State University of New York Press, New York.

Clarke, M. and Voake, C. (1990) *The Best of Aesop's Fables*, Walker Books, London.

Clay, M. (1972) *What Did I Write?*, Heinemann, Auckland.

Cox, K. and Hughes, P. (1990) *Early Years History: An Approach Through Story*, Liverpool Institute of Higher Education, Liverpool.

Creary, C., Storr, T., Tait, M. and Claxton, P. (1991) *Science from Stories*, Northamptonshire Science Resources, Northamptonshire County Council, Northampton.

Dale, P. (1991) *The Elephant Tree*, Walker Books, London.

De'Ath, E. and Pugh, G. (1986) *Working with Parents: A Training Resource Pack*, National Children's Bureau, London.

Department of Education and Science (1967) *Children and their Primary Schools: A Report of the Central Advisory Council for Education (England)*, Volume 1, HMSO, London.

Department of Education and Science (1989a) *Aspects of Primary Education: The Education of Children Under Five*, HMSO, London.

Department of Education and Science (1989b) *Aspects of Primary Education: The Teaching and Learning of Science*, London, HMSO.

Department of Education and Science (1990a) *Starting with Quality: The Report of the Committee of Inquiry into the Quality of Educational Experience Offered to Three- and Four-Year-Olds*, HMSO, London.

Department of Education and Science (1990b) *English in the National Curriculum*, No. 2, HMSO, London.

Department for Education and Employment (1996) *Desirable Outcomes of Nursery Education on Entry to Compulsory Schooling*, HMSO, London.

Department for Education and Employment (1997) *Dearing Review*, HMSO, London.

Department for Education and Employment (1998) The National Literacy Strategegy, DfEE, London.

Design Council (1992) *The Wolf Proof House – Using Stories as Contexts for Design and Technology*, Design Council, London.

Development Education Centre (1991) *Start with a Story – Supporting Young Children's Exploration of Issues*, Development Education Centre, Birmingham.

Dickson, L., Brown, M., and Gibson, O. (1993) *Children Learning Mathematics – a Teacher's Guide to Recent Research*, Cassell, London.

Donaldson, M. (1983) *Children's Minds*, Fontana/Collins, Glasgow.

Dowling, M. (1988) *Education 3 to 5: A Teacher's Handbook*, Paul Chapman Publishing, London.

Drummond, M. J. (1993) *Assessing Children's Learning*, David Fulton Publishers, London.

Drummond, M. J. and Nutbrown, C. (1996) 'Observing and assessing young children', in Pugh, G. (ed.) *Contemporary Issues in the Early Years: Working Collaboratively for Children* (2nd edition), Paul Chapman Publishing/National Children's Bureau, London.

Drummond, M. J., Rouse, D. and Pugh, G. (1992) *Making Assessment Work: Values and Principles in Assessing Young Children's Learning*, NES Arnold/National Children's Bureau, available from Early Childhood Unit, National Children's Bureau, 8 Wakley Street, London, EC1V 7QE.

Early Years Curriculum Group (1992) *First Things First: Educating Young Children – A Guide for Parents and Governors*, Early Years Curriculum Group, Madeleine Lindley Ltd., 79 The Acorn Centre, Oldham OL1 3NE.

Edwards, H. and Niland, D. (1982) *There's a Hippopotamus on our Roof Eating Cake!*, Hodder & Stoughton, London.

Einstein, A. (1920) in Calaprice, A. (1996) *The Quotable Einstein*, Princeton University Press, Princeton, N.J.

Emblen, V. and Schmitz, H. (1991) *Learning Through Story*, Scholastic Publications, Leamington Spa.

Fair, S. (1989) *Barney's Beanstalk*, Macdonald, London.

Flack, M. and Weise, K. (1991) *The Story about Ping*, Random Century, London.

Fontana, D. (1984) *The Education of the Young Child* (2nd edition), Blackwell, London.

Foreman, M. (1989) *Ben's Baby*, Beaver Books, London.

Gardner, H. (1980) *Artful Scribbles – The Significance of Children's Drawings*, Jill Norman, London.

Gentle, K. (1985) *Children and Art Teaching*, Croom Helm, Beckenham.

Goldschmied, E. (1989) 'Playing and learning in the first year of life', in Williams, V. (ed.) *Babies in Daycare: An Examination of the Issues*, Daycare Trust, London.

Goldschmied, E. (1991) 'What to do with the under twos, heuristic play – infants learning', in Rouse, D. (ed.) *Babies and Toddlers: Carers and Educators – Quality for the Under Threes*, National Children's Bureau, London.

Goldschmied, E. and Jackson, S. (1994) *People Under Three in Daycare*, Routledge, London.

Goodman, Y. (1980) The Roots of Literacy, *Claremont, Reading Conference Year Book*, Claremont NJ.

Griffiths, A. and Edmonds, M. (1986) *Report on the Calderdale Pre-School Parent Book Project*, Schools' Psychological Service, Calderdale Education Department, Halifax.

Gura, P. (ed.) (1992) *Exploring Learning – Young Children and Blockplay*, Paul Chapman Publishing, London.

Hannon, P. and Nutbrown, C. (1997) 'Teachers' use of a conceptual framework for early literacy education involving parents', *Teacher Development*, Vol. 1, No. 3, pp. 405–19.

Hannon, P., Weinberger, J. and Nutbrown, C. (1991) 'A study of work with parents to promote early literacy development', *Research Papers in Education*, Vol. 6, No. 2, pp. 77–97.

Hill, E. (1980) *Where's Spot?*, Heinemann, London.

Hirst, K. (1998) Pre-school literacy experiences of children in Punjabi, Urdu and Gujerati speaking families in England, *British Educational Research Journal*, Vol. 24, No. 4, pp. 415–429.

Hissey, J. (1992) *Jolly Snow*, Random Century, London.
Hodgkin, R. A. (1985) *Playing and Exploring, Education through the Discovery of Order*, Methuen, London.
Holt, J. (1991) *Learning All the Time*, Education Now Publishing Co-operative, Ticknall, Derbyshire, Lighthouse Books, Liss, Hants.
House of Commons (1988) *Educational Provision for the Under Fives*, Education, Science and Arts Committee (first report), HMSO, London.
Hughes, S. (1982) *Alfie Gets in First*, Picture Lions, London.
Hughes, S. (1991) *Up and Up*, Red Fox, London.
Hurst, V. and Joseph, J. (1998) *Supporting Early Learning: The Way Forward*, Open University Press, Buckingham.
Hutchins, P. (1969) *Rosie's Walk*, The Bodley Head, London.
Hutchins, P. (1972) *Titch*, The Bodley Head, London.
Inkpen, M. (1991) *The Blue Balloon*, Picture Knight, London.
Isaacs, S. (1948) *Childhood and After*, Routledge & Kegan Paul, London.
Junior Achievement (1991) *Quality Education Begins with Parents*, Junior Achievement of Central Arizona, Phoenix, Ariz.
Lear, E. and Cooper, H. (1991) *The Owl and the Pussycat*, Hamish Hamilton, London.
Lloyd, D. and Dale, P. (1986) *The Stop Watch*, Walker Books, London.
Lloyd, D. and Rees, M. (1991) *The Ball*, Walker Books, London.
Lujan, M. E., Stolworthy, D. L. and Wooden, S. L. (1986) *A Parent Training Early Intervention Programme in Preschool Literacy*, ERIC (Educational Resources Information Centre), descriptive report, ED 270 988.
Maris, R. (1990) *Hold Tight, Bear!*, Walker Books, London.
Mark, J. and Voake, C. (1986) *Fur*, Walker Books, London.
Mason, L. (1989) *A Book of Boxes*, Orchard Books, London.
Matthews, G. (1984) 'Learning and teaching mathematical skills', in Fontana, D. (ed.) *The Education of the Young Child* (2nd edition), Blackwell, London.
Matthews, J. (1994) *Helping Children to Draw and Paint in Early Childhood: Children's Visual Representation*, Hodder & Stoughton, London.
McKee, D. (1989) *Elmer*, Andersen Press, London.
Meade, A. and Cubey, P. (1995) *Thinking Children: Learning About Schemas*, New Zealand Council for Educational Research and Institute for Early Childhood Studies, Wellington College of Education/Victoria University of Wellington.
Meek, M. (1988) *How Texts Teach what Readers Learn*, The Thimble Press, Stroud.
Miko, I. (1993) *Little Lumpty*, Walker, London.
Mort, L. and Morris, J. (1991) *Starting with Rhyme*, Scholastic Publications, Leamington Spa.
Moyles, J. (1989) *Just Playing? The role and status of play in early childhood education*, Open University Press, Milton Keynes.
Murphy, J. (1982) *On the Way Home*, Pan Macmillan Children's Books, London.
National Writing Project (1989) *Becoming a Writer*, Nelson, Walton-on-Thames.
Nicholls, R. (ed.) with Sedgewick, J., Duncan, J., Curwin, L. and McDougall, B. (1986) *Rumpus Schema Extra: Teachers in Education*, Cleveland LEA, Cleveland.
Nister, E. (1981) *The Magic Window*, HarperCollins, Glasgow.
Nutbrown, C. (1994) 'Young children in educational establishments', in David, T. (ed.) *Working Together for Young Children*, Routledge, London.
Nutbrown, C. (1996) *Respectful Educators – Capable Learner: Children's Rights and Early Education*, Paul Chapman Publishing, London.
Nutbrown, C. (1997) *Recognising Early Literacy Development: Assessing Children's Achievement*, Paul Chapman Publishing, London.
Nutbrown, C. (1998) *The Lore and Language of Early Education*, USDE Publications, University of Sheffield. Available from the Department of Educational Studies, University of Sheffield, 388 Glossop Road, Sheffield S10 2JA.

Nutbrown, C. and Hannon, P. (1997) *Preparing for Early Literacy Education with Parents* – a professional development manual, REAL Project NES Arnold, Nottingham.

Nutbrown, C. and Hirst, K. (eds.) (1993) *Using Stories to Stimulate Scientific and Technological Learning and Development with Children under Five*, City of Sheffield LEA, Sheffield.

Nutbrown, C. and Swift, G. (eds.) (1993) *The Learning and Development of 3–5 Year Olds, Schema Observations* (2nd edition) City of Sheffield Education Department, Sheffield.

Nutbrown, C., Hannon, P. and Weinberger, J. (1991) 'Training teachers to work with parents to promote early literacy development', *International Journal of Early Childhood*, Vol. 23, No. 2, pp. 1–10.

Oldham LEA (1992) *Writing for All*, Oldham LEA, Oldham.

Paley, V. G. (1981) *Wally's Stories: Conversations in the Kindergarten*, Harvard University Press, Cambridge, Mass.

Payton, S. (1984) 'Developing an Awareness of Print: A Young Child's First Steps Towards Literacy', *Educational Review*, No. 2, Birmingham University, Birmingham.

Pearce, P. (1958) *Tom's Midnight Garden*, Oxford University Press, Oxford.

Pearce, P. (1987) *The Tooth Ball*, Picture Puffins, Harmondsworth.

Pen Green Centre for Under Fives and their Families (no date) *A Schema Booklet for Parents*, Pen Green Centre, Corby.

Piaget, J. (1953) *The Origin of Intelligence in the Child*, Routledge & Kegan Paul, London.

Piaget, J. (1972) 'Development and learning', in Stendler-Lavatelli, C. and Stendler, F. (eds) *Readings in Child Behavior and Development* (3rd edition), Harcourt Brace Janovich, New York.

Piaget, J. and Inhelder, B. (1956) *The Child's Conception of Space*, Routledge & Kegan Paul, London.

Pienkowski, J. (1980) *Dinner Time*, Gallery Five, London.

Pienkowski, J. (1986) *Fancy That!*, Orchard Books, London.

Plaskow, D. (ed.) (1967) *The Crucial Years*, Society for Education through Art, London.

Prater, J. (1987) *The Gift*, Puffin, Harmondsworth.

Preschool Playgroups Association (1991) *What Children Learn in Playgroup: A Guide to the Curriculum*, Preschool Playgroups Association, London.

Qualifications and Curriculum Authority (1997), *Baseline Assessment Scales*, QCA, London.

Roberts, R. (1995) *Self-esteem and successful early learning*, Hodder & Stoughton, London.

Roffey, M. (1982) *Home Sweet Home*, Piper, London.

Rosen, M. and Oxenbury, H. (1989) *We're Going on a Bear Hunt*, Walker Books, London.

Rouse, D. (ed.) (1990) *Babies and Toddlers: Carers and Educators – Quality for the Under Threes*, National Children's Bureau, London.

Rouse, D. and Griffin, S. (1992) 'Quality for the under threes', in Pugh, G. (ed.) *Contemporary Issues in the Early Years: Working Collaboratively for Children*, Paul Chapman Publishing/National Children's Bureau, London.

Samuels, V. (1991) *Boxed In*, Red Fox, London.

Schickedanz, J. (1990) *Adam's Righting Revolutions – One Child's Literacy Development from Infancy through Grade One*, Heinemann, Portsmouth, NH.

Schiller, C. (1979) *Christian Schiller in his Own Words*, National Association for Primary Education/A & C Black, London.

Schools Curriculum and Assessment Authority (1996) *Baseline Assessment – Draft Proposals*, SCAA, London.

Schools Curriculum and Assessment Authority (1997), *The National Framework for Baseline Assessment*, SCAA, London.

Sendak, M. (1967) *Where the Wild Things Are*, The Bodley Head, London.

Shapur, F. (1991) *The Rainbow Balloon*, Simon & Schuster, London.

Sheffield Early Years Literacy Association (1990) *Reading Writing and Classroom Reality*, Sheffield Early Years Literacy Association, Sheffield.

Sheffield LEA (1988) *Dynamic Vertical Schema: Thoughts, Observations, Resources*, City of Sheffield Education Department, Sheffield.

Sheffield LEA (1989) *Enveloping and Containing Schema: Thoughts, Observations, Resources*, City of Sheffield Education Department, Sheffield.

Sheldon, D. and Smith, W. (1991) *A Witch Got on at Paddington Station*, Red Fox, London.

Sieveking, A. and Lincoln, F. (1989) *What's Inside?*, Frances Lincoln, London.

Smail, D. (1984) *Taking Care: An Alternative to Therapy*, Dent, London.

Smith, T. (1980) *Parents and Preschool: Oxford Preschool Research Project*, Grant McIntyre, London.

Stendler-Lavatelli, C. and Stendler, F. (1972) *Readings in Child Behavior and Development* (3rd edition) Harcourt Brace Janovich, New York.

Stenhouse, L. (1975) *An Introduction to Curriculum Research and Development*, Heinemann, London.

Tait, M. and Roberts, R. (1974) *Play, Language and Experience*, OMEP, London.

Tinbergen, N. (1976) *The Importance of Being Playful*, British Association for Early Childhood Education, London.

Vygotsky, L. S. (1978) *Mind in Society*, Harvard University Press, Cambridge, Mass.

Waterland, L. (1985) *Read with Me – An Apprenticeship Approach to Reading*, The Thimble Press, London.

Waterland, L. (1992) 'Ranging freely: the why and the what of real books', in Styles, M., Bearne, E. and Watson, V. (eds) *After Alice – Exploring Children's Literature*, Cassell, London.

Watson, V. (1992) 'Irresponsible writers and responsible readers', in Styles, M., Bearne, E. and Watson, V. (eds) *After Alice – Exploring Children's Literature*, Cassell, London.

Weinberger, J. (1996) *Literacy goes to School*, Paul Chapman Publishing, London.

Whalley, M. (1995) *Learning to be Strong*, Hodder & Stoughton, London.

Wild, M. and Huxley, D. (1990) *Mr Nick's Knitting*, Picture Knight, London.

Wilhelm, H. (1985) *I'll Always Love You*, Hodder & Stoughton, London.

Williams, M. (1988) *Noah's Ark*, Walker Books, London.

Williams, M. (1990) *Joseph and his Magnificent Coat of Many Colours*, Walker Books, London.

Williams, T. (ed.) (1991) *Stories as Starting Points for Design and Technology*, Design Council, London.

Willis, V. (1991) *The Secret in the Matchbox*, Picture Corgi, London.

Winter, M. and Rouse, J. (1990) 'Fostering intergenerational literacy: The Mossouri Parents as Teachers Programme', *The Reading Teacher*, Vol. 24, No. 2, pp. 382–6.

Wray, D., Bloom, W. and Hall, N. (1989) *Literacy in Action*, Falmer Press, London.

Zelinsky, P. (1990) *The Wheels on the Bus*, Orchard Books, London.

Zion, G. and Bloy Graham, M. (1960) *Harry the Dirty Dog*, The Bodley Head, London.

AUTHOR INDEX

SUBJECT INDEX